I0188989

A CENTURY OF SPORTS
AT THE UNIVERSITY OF
NEBRASKA AT KEARNEY

Most of the photographs in this book come from the Donald K. Briggs Collection, a voluminous collection of photographs, negatives, and memorabilia that chronicles Antelope athletics specifically and the history of the campus generally. Housed at the Calvin T. Ryan Library on the University of Nebraska at Kearney campus, this collection was invaluable in putting together this book. Pictured here is Don Briggs, or "Mr. B" as he is affectionately known around the University of Nebraska at Kearney Athletic Department. For his meritorious service to the University of Nebraska at Kearney and to the athletic department, Briggs has been awarded the Distinguished Alumni Service Award (1984), and he was inducted into the National Association of Intercollegiate Athletics Hall of Fame and the University of Nebraska at Kearney Athletic Hall of Fame.

On the front cover: Please see page 22. (Donald K. Briggs Collection, Calvin T. Ryan Library, University of Nebraska at Kearney.)

On the back cover: Please see page 10. (Donald K. Briggs Collection, Calvin T. Ryan Library, University of Nebraska at Kearney.)

Cover background: Please see pages 16 and 17. (Donald K. Briggs Collection, Calvin T. Ryan Library, University of Nebraska at Kearney.)

A CENTURY OF SPORTS AT THE UNIVERSITY OF NEBRASKA AT KEARNEY

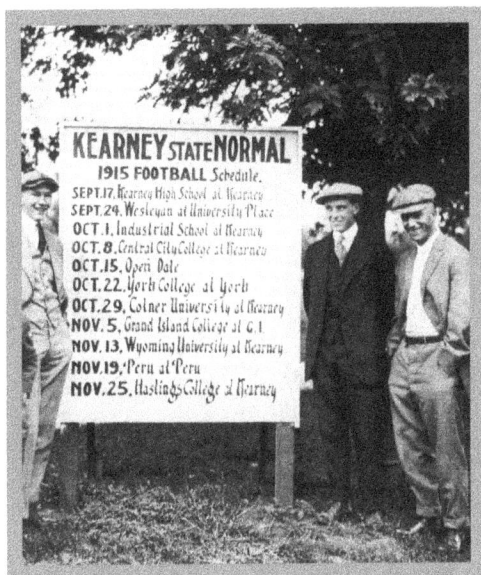

Mark R. Ellis and Jordan T. Kuck

ARCADIA
PUBLISHING

Copyright © 2007 by Mark R. Ellis and Jordan T. Kuck
ISBN 978-1-5316-3160-4

Published by Arcadia Publishing
Charleston SC, Chicago IL, Portsmouth NH, San Francisco CA

Library of Congress Catalog Card Number: 2007927178

For all general information contact Arcadia Publishing at:
Telephone 843-853-2070
Fax 843-853-0044
E-mail sales@arcadiapublishing.com
For customer service and orders:
Toll-Free 1-888-313-2665

Visit us on the Internet at www.arcadiapublishing.com

This book is dedicated to the Blue and Gold faithful.

CONTENTS

Acknowledgments   6

Introduction   7

1.   The Early Years: 1905–1922   9

2.   The Fulmer Era: 1922–1945   29

3.   The Foster Era, Part I: 1945–1971   49

4.   The Foster Era, Part II: 1945–1971   77

5.   The Modern Era: 1971–2007   103

ACKNOWLEDGMENTS

Many people have contributed greatly and aided us in the completion of this book. Thus, we would like to thank Don Briggs; the University of Nebraska at Kearney Athletic Department, especially Peter Yazvac; John Lillis and the entire Calvin T. Ryan Library staff; Guy and Cheryl Murray; Mary Iten; and Tom Kropp. We also owe a special thanks to coach Tom Osborne, Dr. L. R. Smith, Bryce Abbey, coach Jerry Stine, Mike Ford, the janitors at Eustis-Farnam Community School, and Pam Proskocil. They have all been most helpful, and, of course, any and all errors are only due to our own shortcomings.

INTRODUCTION

For more than 100 years, students at the University of Nebraska at Kearney (formerly the Nebraska State Normal School, Nebraska State Teachers College, Kearney State Teachers College, and Kearney State College) have been putting on the blue and gold and taking to the gridiron, hardwood, diamond, and cinder track. In 1910, after five years of competing without an official school mascot, the student body chose the antelope because it symbolized "strength, swiftness, and the ability to adapt to adverse conditions." That definition of an antelope, as the pages in this book will reveal, has come to define Kearney's sports program and the athletes who have competed in the blue and gold.

The book is organized into five main chapters, which are roughly matched to the corresponding dominant personalities of the era. The first chapter covers the time period between the founding of the school in 1905 and the hiring of Fred Fulmer 1922. In this section we highlight, for instance, the 1911 baseball team that brought home the school's first ever championship. We have also tried to reawaken the long-forgotten accomplishments of coach George Van Buren, who, for all intents and purposes, is the founding father of University of Nebraska at Kearney (UNK) athletics.

Chapter 2 centers on the Fred Fulmer era, with a significant amount of time also devoted to the achievements of coach L. F. "Pop" Klein. During this period, future UNK Athletic Hall of Fame athletes such as Adolph "Pat" Panek, Frank Lydic, Carl and Clyde Cox, Paul Blessing, Ihling "Brick" Carskadon, James Lovell, and Frank Dusek competed for the Antelopes. Lesser-known but equally gifted athletes such as George and Rex Reed, Ronald Lewis, and Lloyd McCullough also represented the Antelopes but have yet to be inducted into the UNK Athletic Hall of Fame. Despite the talent-laden teams of the 1920s, Fulmer produced only one basketball championship (1928) and two cross-country titles (1928 and 1929). Between 1930 and 1943, however, the Antelopes produced a number of conference championship teams.

The two subsequent chapters highlight the days of coach Charlie Foster. During the Foster era, championships in football, track, and cross-country were commonplace. For example, in chapter 3, we highlight Foster's impressive string of conference track championships between 1955 and 1971. Equally striking is the fact that his cross-country teams ran away with 12 straight conference titles between 1956 and 1967. Due to the wealth of archival photographs and information, the football program has been given its own space in chapter 4. In this chapter, we examine the emergence of a championship football program under coach Allen Zikmund, who captured 11 conference championships in 17 seasons.

Finally, in chapter 5, we conclude with the modern era, which covers 1971 to 2007. Most noteworthy here is the development of women's sports and other sports that have become a tradition at UNK. As a sample, we have included the history of UNK's storied volleyball team and the powerhouse wrestling program. We also look at star athletes like Erin Gudmundson, Susan Johnson, Beth Stuart, Ali Amiri-Eliasi, and others.

In a book of this size, it is impossible to highlight every athlete and coach. After all, in football alone nearly 2,000 athletes have lettered since 1905. As a consequence, many Antelope greats who deserve to be in this book are not. One reason why an athlete might not have made it into these pages was a lack of a photograph. Photographs are hard to come by for the pre-1950 period and the years between 1970 and 1990. The careful reader might also notice that we gave the pre-1971 era more attention than the modern era. As historians we were inclined to research the historical development of Antelope athletics, particularly during the success-filled Foster era. To the athletes we left out, or the sports that received limited attention, we apologize. Of course, any mistakes in fact or interpretation are solely those of the authors.

In terms of All-Americans, a disclaimer should be noted. We discovered that the archival materials, although plentiful and useful, sometimes contradicted the official records. The National Association of Intercollegiate Athletics (NAIA) and National Collegiate Athletic Association (NCAA), for example, do not recognize those on the honorable mention list as All-Americans, yet it appears as if the archival materials are just the opposite. Thus, for the sake of clarity, we have included those on the honorable mention list in our discussion of All-Americans.

One purpose of this book is to recognize the early athletes and coaches who built the Antelope athletic program into the powerhouse that it is today. Most of the names of athletes and coaches from the pre-1920 period have been long forgotten. Coach George Van Buren, for example, is remembered by few outside those who have studied the school's sports history. A host of exceptional athletes who competed for the Antelopes during this period have been dealt the same fate. Earl "Irish" Carrig, for example, was a four-year starter at quarterback, earning all-state honors each year he competed. He was also the catcher and an accomplished hitter on the 1911 championship baseball team. Russell "Red" Burford was a brawny all-state center who in 1911 captained the Antelope football squad. The *Lincoln Journal* boasted that Burford was the best center in the state, if not the best football player in the state. Another Antelope standout was Bob Randolph, who after playing for the Antelope football squad joined Northwestern University's football team. In 1916, Randolph was Northwestern's team captain, and he was recognized as one of the best players in the nation. Thus it is our hope that perhaps we can recognize a number of athletes from long ago who have not been given their rightful place in the UNK Athletic Hall of Fame. To our readers, we offer, as a conclusion to this introduction, a poem reminiscent of those sports-related poems that were written long ago.

A Tale of Old
From Carrig to Kropp, we've seen them all
To Kearney they come, to both win and fall.
One hundred years it's been, since the days of old
And thus it must be, that the story be told,
Of how Lydic ran and Butolph threw
All while donning the gold and blue.
To the reader, then, we invite you to see
A century of sports in the great town of Kear-ney.

1

THE EARLY YEARS

1905–1922

The origins of athletics at Kearney date back to 1905, the year that the Nebraska State Normal School at Kearney (sometimes called the Western State Normal in the early days) opened its doors to students. Looking back, sports had a humble beginning. During the school's first few years, athletes on the football, basketball, and baseball teams were coached by college faculty and played mostly against local high schools. The arrival of George Van Buren in 1910 lifted the Blue and Gold athletic program to new heights. During his four-year stint in Kearney, Van Buren laid the groundwork for the foundation of a modern-day athletic program. Using his experience and skills as a standout athlete at Cornell College in Iowa, Van Buren elevated the Antelopes to a level that saw them competing for conference championships and earning spots on all-state teams. Guided by Van Buren, and armed with the antelope as their mascot, the 1911 baseball team slugged its way to the school's first championship. The 1911 football team, after losing to the Nebraska Cornhuskers by a score of 117-0, stormed through the conference but fell short of winning the conference title after losing 6-3 to Peru Normal. Under Van Buren, the women's basketball team also saw changes as it began competing against other colleges and, on occasion, playing by the men's rules.

When Van Buren left Kearney in 1914, the Antelopes were respected throughout Nebraska as a tough competitor that produced high-caliber athletes. The advances made by Van Buren were nullified by World War I. Due to the departure of men and funding, sports teams were thinned out and suffered through consecutive losing seasons. But with the birth of a new decade and an influx of returning men, the sports teams appeared to have a bright future.

Baseball was first played at Kearney in the summer of 1906. Coached by O. W. Neale, the 1906 team finished with an 8-1 record, mostly against local town teams. The program continued its early success in the ensuing years, finishing the next three seasons with a combined 36-10 record. Pictured here are the 1907 team members wearing uniforms that indicate that they played for the Western State Normal School. This photograph was taken on the steps of the old administration building.

George Van Buren, a renowned multisport star at Cornell College in Iowa, was hired in September 1910 to head the Antelope athletic program. He lifted the normal school's athletic program to a level of competitiveness. Prior to his arrival, high schools regularly handed Kearney humiliating defeats while college teams viewed games against the Antelopes as a warm-up for more legitimate competition. Upon departing in 1914, Van Buren left Kearney with a powerhouse baseball and football program and a basketball team that had its own gymnasium and competed at the collegiate level.

THE EARLY YEARS

When Van Buren took over coaching duties in 1910, the Antelopes joined the athletic association comprised of Peru Normal, Grand Island Baptist Collage, Hastings College, York College, Doane College, Wesleyan College, Cotner College, Bellevue College, and Central City College. Pictured here is Van Buren with his 1911 championship team. The team was led by Earl Carrig, a three-sport standout for the Antelopes and the team's best all-around player. Carrig's batting prowess was such that his 1913 season was cut short when he signed for the summer with a professional team out of Streeter, Illinois.

Despite having winning seasons and a championship in 1911, when money became tight, baseball was the first sport to be disbanded. Although a team was thrown together for several games in 1916, continued financial difficulties and the strains of World War I put an end to Antelope baseball. Although America's pastime sporadically showed up on campus, as a number of times a team was fielded to take on local town teams, intercollegiate baseball was not reinstated until 1961. Pictured here is one of the last teams fielded.

The school's first playing field was shared by both the football and baseball teams. Athletic Park, as it was known, ran east to west, stretching from the present-day student affairs building on the northeast, past Otto Olsen on the northwest, and south to present-day Highway 30. A board fence surrounded the playing field. Although a grandstand stood on the north edge of the field, automobiles frequently lined the field for both football and baseball games. The photograph above shows the grandstands that were situated on the north side of the field. Green Terrace, the first dormitory, is visible just beyond the playing field. Posing in front of the grandstand, below, is the 1906 football squad.

For the first six seasons, the basketball team did not have a gymnasium, and thus they were forced to practice in a classroom. Conditions were little better when it came to game time, as the team had to play its games in the city armory. Pictured here is the 1908 basketball squad. Prof. A. J. Mercer, who organized and coached many of Kearney's earliest sports teams, is standing at the far left.

Coach George Van Buren put together a longer and more rigorous basketball schedule that included games against other colleges. Accordingly the 1913 team finished with an 8-3 record, including a victory against Cotner College, the basketball powerhouse of Nebraska. Men's basketball, not unlike the other sports, suffered a severe blow when Van Buren departed and from the hardships brought about by World War I. The men's program hit its low point in 1919 when, even though the school had a brand-new gymnasium, the season was cancelled due to a postwar-related lack of funds. Pictured above is the 1911 squad.

In the fall of 1905, Prof. Wynfred E. Allen organized a women's basketball team. The "Teddy Bears," as they were affectionately nicknamed, played five games that season, mostly against high schools. The games were as much a social event as anything. For example, in 1906, the women's basketball team hosted a game at the city armory against Peru Normal, losing 26-16. After the game, the women held a reception in the chapel for the visiting team, complete with readings, music, entertainment, food, and drinks. Pictured here is the 1908 women's team, coached by Prof. Grace Hamer.

George Van Buren tried to enhance the women's basketball team by strengthening the schedule and organizing doubleheaders alongside the men's game. Oftentimes the women's team would play by the men's rules in the first half and the women's rules in the second half. In the women's game there were six players who were split into three smaller "courts," and no player could leave her designated court. The women's basketball program disappeared just before World War I and did not reappear until the 1960s.

Early on, winter sports were difficult due to the lack of a gymnasium. In 1911, under the supervision of Van Buren, the athletes built the first gymnasium just east of Green Terrace Hall. "The Barn," as it became lovingly called, was a wooden building, 60 by 80 feet, with a dirt basketball court, a practice baseball field, and a 75-yard cinder track. During basketball season, truckloads of hay bales were brought in for seating, while new oil stoves provided heat.

The Barn was torn down in 1916 when the college began construction of a new, state-of-the-art gymnasium. Construction of the new gymnasium (now Copeland Hall) was, however, disrupted by World War I. With manpower and materials being diverted to the war effort, the gymnasium was not finished until late 1918. Once completed, the three-story brick building was the pride of the campus. On the first floor was a calisthenics room, a swimming pool, and locker rooms, while the gymnasium was housed on the second floor.

Professors Wynfred E. Allen and A. J. Mercer organized the university's first football team in October 1905. Lacking experience and a trained coach, the team struggled its first year and finished the season scoreless with a 0-5-1 record against local high school competition. In 1906, a dirt field with grandstands was erected, and the team finished its more successful second season

with a record of 3-4-2, scoring a season total of 28 points. Pictured is the 1906 team that earned the school's first victory with a 6-0 win over Lexington High School. The 1906 team also played the school's first-ever game against Hastings College. The 10-4 loss initiated a rivalry between the two central Nebraska schools that would burn with intensity until the late 1960s.

The 1907 football team, pictured above, was coached by George Porter, an English literature professor. During this period, the gridiron boys began to play more college teams. In 1907, they beat Grand Island Business College 5-0 but lost to Doane College 18-0. In 1908, Hastings College handed the normal boys their most humiliating loss, a 45-0 defeat that fueled the fire of the growing rivalry. With such lopsided losses, and a team depleted by injuries, the 1908 season was cancelled after just three games.

By 1910, the *Kearney Hub* and the college newspaper, the *Antelope*, began to follow football with interest, and as a result, the first football "stars" began to emerge. Pictured here are the veteran players of the 1909 squad. From left to right are Harry Dryden (all-state tackle in 1910), Lynn Hoyt, Nelson Cool, and Guy Sampson. In the coming years, standouts such as Russell "Red" Burford, Earl "Irish" Carrig, Bob Randolph, Charles "Chick" Wareham, and Dutch Heider would lead the Antelopes on the gridiron.

THE EARLY YEARS

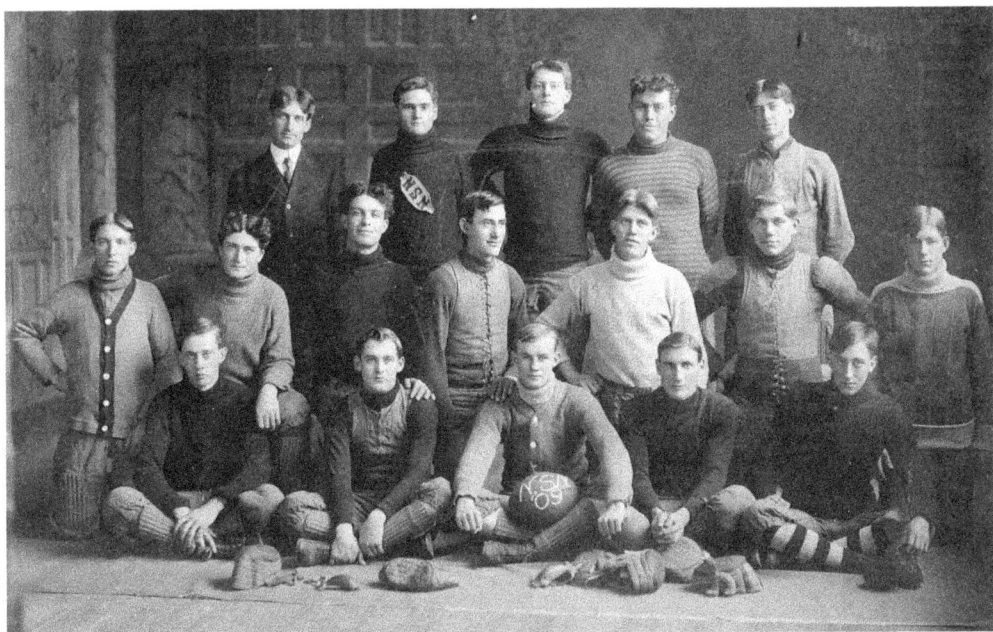

Although the 1909 season only produced a 1-3-2 record, including another loss to Hastings College, Kearney's schedule now consisted primarily of games against other colleges, including Peru, Grand Island Baptist, Doane, and Hastings. Pictured here is the 1909 football squad. Russell Burford (center of back row) emerged as a standout center who later gained statewide notoriety for his physical play.

Clowning around in the snow is the 1909 football squad. The photograph was taken in downtown Kearney on the south side of Twenty-second Street between Central Avenue and First Avenue.

Pictured here are two of the earliest-known football action shots. The photograph above is the 1907 Thanksgiving Day game against Doane College. Kearney lost the game 18-0. The original football field ran west to east and was surrounded by a 10-foot-high board fence. In the background is the original administration building before any additions were built. Pictured below is the opening kickoff of the 1910 game against Doane College. The game was a hard-fought defensive battle, but Kearney went down by a score of 3-0. By 1910, the administration building had been expanded.

School spirit permeated the student body, faculty, and administration at Nebraska State Normal School at Kearney. If not representing the Antelopes on the field, one was expected to show school spirit by purchasing a season ticket, learning the fight songs, and participating in halftime activities. In the photograph above, students and fans perform a snake dance on the field during halftime festivities, while university president George S. Dick (at right) watches a game with students.

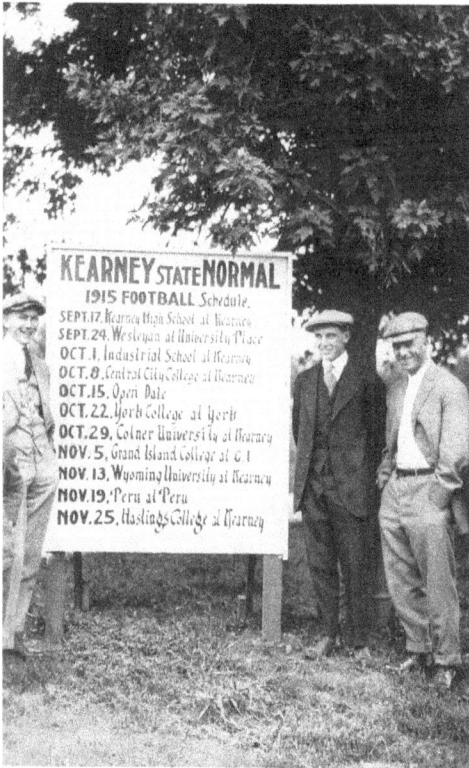

KEARNEY STATE NORMAL
1915 FOOTBALL Schedule.
SEPT.17. Kearney High School at Kearney
SEPT.24. Wesleyan at University Place
OCT.1. Industrial School at Kearney
OCT.8. Central City College at Kearney
OCT.15. Open Date
OCT.22. York College at York
OCT.29. Cotner University at Kearney
NOV.5. Grand Island College at G.I.
NOV.13. Wyoming University at Kearney
NOV.19. Peru at Peru
NOV.25. Hastings College at Kearney

During the first 10 years of the football program, the team played a wide variety of opponents, including local high schools such as Kearney High School, the Boys Industrial School (reform school), the Kearney Military Academy, other normal schools such as Peru and Northern Colorado, colleges that no longer exist such as Central City College and Grand Island Baptist College, private colleges such as Wesleyan, Doane, and York, and state universities such as Nebraska and Wyoming. Here members of the 1915 football team proudly display the year's schedule on a campus billboard. Coached by Harry Tollefsen and led by players such as Earl "Irish" Carrig and Dutch Heider, the 1915 Antelopes posted a 6-1-1 record.

The Antelopes squared off against the Kearney Military Academy five times between 1905 and 1910. The military boys always put up a good fight, winning by a score of 11-0 in 1905 and drawing a 6-6 tie in 1906. This photograph was snapped after the Antelopes defeated the military academy 29-0 in 1910. Notice that the Kearney Military Academy team was racially integrated, highly unusual in 1910. The first African American did not put on the blue and gold for the Antelopes until the 1950s.

Perhaps the close proximity of the two schools fueled the fire of the oftentimes-bitter rivalry with Hastings College. Hastings won the first four meetings, but beginning in 1910, with coach George Van Buren at the helm, the Antelopes began to match the play of their archrivals. Under Van Buren, the Antelopes beat the Broncos three consecutive years between 1911 and 1913. After the 1911 game in Kearney, the Hastings coach complained that his team had been forced to eat at the Palace Café, which he claimed was not "fit for a dog to eat in." Beyond wins, losses, and bragging rights, both schools believed they were treated poorly by the opposing community.

Sending the team off on the road became a school tradition. After holding a pep rally in the auditorium, the student body and band paraded their athletes to the train depot. When the 1911 squad left for Peru, hundreds of students gathered around the train. Fifteen football players climbed aboard and stood on the rear platform as the crowd chanted the school's fight songs. Captain Russell Burford was presented with a lucky rabbit's foot, a practice that was repeated before every game.

The 1911 football season was one of the most memorable in school history. In 1911, coach George Van Buren's football team produced a 5-3 record, the first winning campaign for the Antelopes. The season was highlighted with wins against Cotner College, Grand Island Business College, and Nebraska Central College. The most rewarding win, however, was a 9-0 victory against Hastings College, the first win in school history against the Broncos. Despite the winning record, the Antelopes suffered their worst defeat in school history when the Nebraska Cornhuskers pummeled the Antelopes in Lincoln by a score of 117-0.

After starring on the gridiron at Kearney High School, Earl "Irish" Carrig joined the Antelopes in 1911, earning the starting position as quarterback and kicker. Carrig was an agile quarterback who used his speed to get around the ends rather than smashing through the defensive front. Carrig's kicking prowess also helped make him the leading scorer in the league. After playing three seasons of football and baseball, Carrig left Kearney to play professional baseball in 1913. He returned in 1915 and once again took over the quarterbacking duties during his final year with the Antelopes.

THE EARLY YEARS

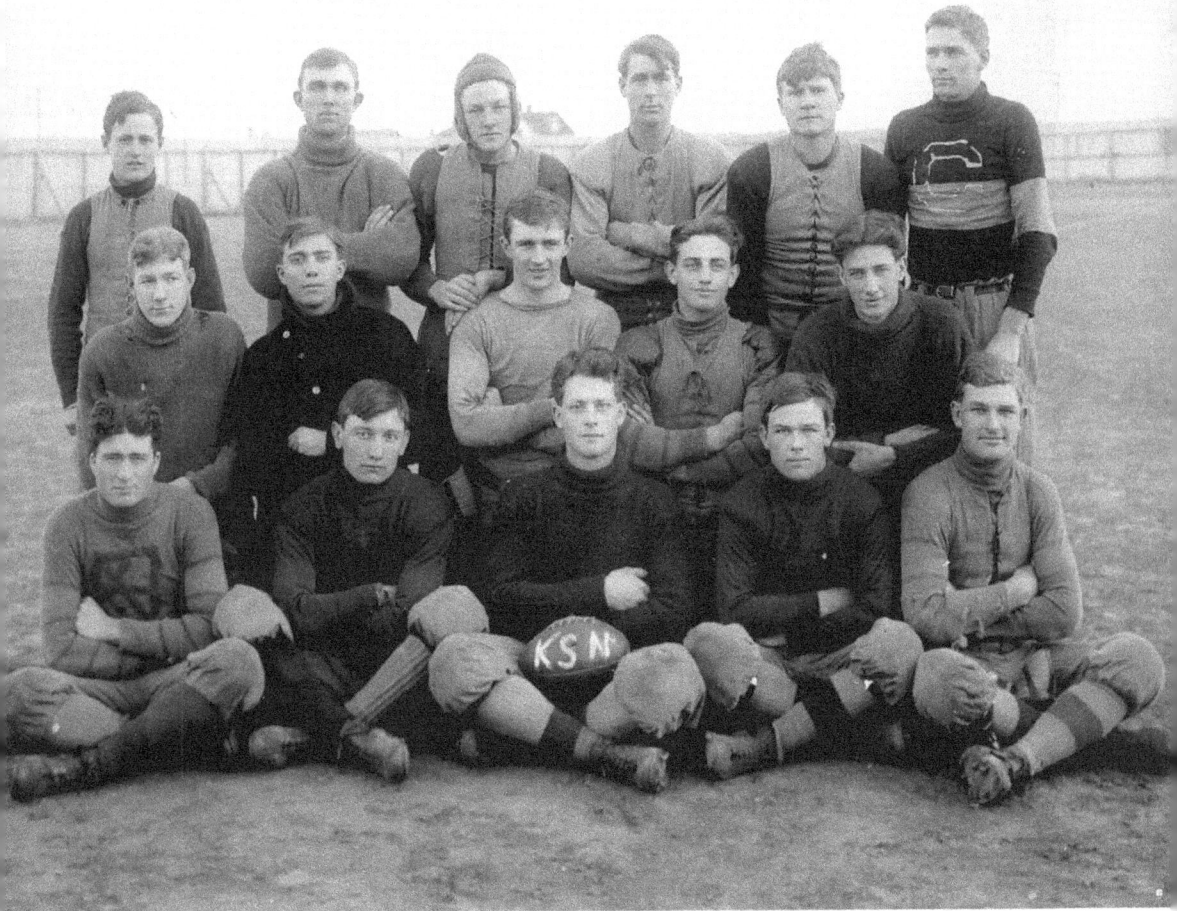

Pictured here is the 1911 squad. From left to right are (first row) Harry Dryden, William "the Flying Dutchman" Birkelbach, Russell "Red" Burford (team captain), William Randolph, and Bob Randolph; (second row) Lawrence Brown, Ralph Essert, Earl "Irish" Carrig, J. Edward Schott, and Milton Dossett; (third row) Charles "Chick" Wareham, Jesse Randolph, "Doc" Cameron, Walter Mary, Ray Campbell, and coach George Van Buren. The 1911 team was led by senior captain Russell "Red" Burford, who was considered by football critics to be the best center in the state, if not the best football player in the state, and freshman quarterback Carrig could punt the ball over 60 yards and led the state in points scored. Both Burford and Carrig were selected to the all-state football team. Another notable player was Bob Randolph, who, after playing four years for the Antelopes, went on to captain the Northwestern University squad (eligibility rules were not as strict in the early 1900s).

In this photograph, senior quarterback Earl Carrig drops back to throw a pass. Before 1911, passing was rare in football because an incomplete pass resulted in a 15-yard penalty. In 1911, rule changes encouraged the pass by abolishing the penalty for an incompletion. This change eliminated much of the "line smashing" of the running game and required more speed and skill. Coach George Van Buren, therefore, put the football in the hands of the smaller but speedier Carrig, who quarterbacked all four years he played for the Antelopes.

Varsity athletes who performed admirably on the field, court, track, or diamond were awarded a K to sew on a sweater. The first sweaters were awarded to the 1911 football team for its "great deeds on the gridiron." The K-Club raised money to host high school tournaments, purchase sweaters for letter winners, and pay for travel expenses. Members of the K-Club also maintained a trophy room and began the practice of displaying photographs of all letter winners. Many of these can still be viewed in the hallways of Cushing Coliseum.

Between 1905 and 1930, the football field ran west to east, with a grandstand along the northern edge. Back then, athletes did not have the luxury of playing on grass, let alone field turf. Long days of practice and little rainfall during the summer produced a hard, rough-and-tumble dirt field. In this picture, the Antelopes, led by quarterback Earl Carrig, are in enemy territory and driving toward the east end zone.

Van Buren compiled an 18-12-1 record during his four seasons as football coach and guided the Kearney boys to three victories against rival Hastings College, including a 40-0 walloping during the 1912 campaign. After Van Buren left in 1914, the program steadily declined. Between 1914 and 1921, four coaches—Harry Tollefsen, W. D. Reynolds, Hugo Otoupalik, and Ray Ozum—combined for a 21-26-3 record. The 1920 squad, pictured here, managed to score only six points the entire season and suffered the college's second-worst defeat in school history when the Peru Bobcats clobbered the Antelopes 103-0.

Coach George Van Buren passionately spent his time advocating the development of a year-round sports program. As a result, in 1911, the first track team made its debut. That spring the six-man track team competed in the Nebraska Collegiate Athletic Association meet held at Wesleyan. The track program, however, was suspended due to financial difficulties in 1914. The annual high school track meet hosted at Kearney, started by Van Buren in 1911, became a campus tradition that still exists today.

Tennis has always been a part of athletic life at Kearney, even though it has not always been viewed as a competitive sport. Tennis was first organized as a sporting activity on campus in 1910, but it had a sporadic existence. One of the barriers for tennis was the maintenance of the courts. Each winter and spring, the courts were nearly destroyed by the harsh, windy Nebraska weather, and if tennis was to be played it was up to the students to resurface the courts.

2

THE FULMER ERA

1922-1945

Fred Fulmer arrived on campus in 1922 after coaching and mentoring for a number of years at YMCA locations in Colorado and Iowa. In addition to coaching football and basketball, Fulmer reintroduced track and field, which had been dormant since before World War I, and in 1928, he added cross-country as an intercollegiate sport. Fulmer coached every sport during the 1920s. His early teams were dominated by individual stars, which translated to little team success. With standouts like Adolph "Pat" Panek, brothers George and Rex Reed and Clyde and Carl Cox, Merle Trail, Frank Lydic, and Ihling "Brick" Carskadon, the decade was dictated by individual stars.

Only the 1927–1928 basketball team and the 1928 and 1929 cross-country teams won championships during Fulmer's tenure. The 1930s and early 1940s, however, developed as a most successful period after Fulmer made a number of important hires. Beginning with the arrival of coach Ted James in 1930, and furthered by the tenure of coach L. F. "Pop" Klein, who arrived in 1935, the school began to more consistently win championships. Winning football championships in 1930, 1936, 1941, and 1942, track championships in 1931, 1932, 1933, 1936, 1939, 1941, 1942, and 1943, golf championships in 1939 and 1940, a basketball championship in 1943, and a tennis championship in 1940, the athletic program was on the brink of consistency when World War II brought athletics to a halt. By the end of the spring semester in 1943, over 300 Kearney boys were serving in the armed forces.

Fred Fulmer was the face of Antelope athletics during the 1920s. Although he coached every sport, basketball is where he excelled. Before Fulmer arrived in 1922, no basketball coach had better than a .500 career winning percentage. Losing seasons, however, were a thing of the past with Fulmer at the helm. During his 10-year stint (1923–1930 and 1933–1935), Fulmer produced a 96-52 record and won a conference championship in 1928. A beloved coach, Fulmer was known for his famous quotes such as "Get in there and fight, but play the game!" and "A winner never quits and a quitter never wins." Fulmer was inducted into the University of Nebraska at Kearney (UNK) Athletic Hall of Fame in 1980.

Adolph "Pat" Panek was the first athlete in school history to win three letters in an academic year. A star running back and kicker in football, the best defender in basketball, and a pole vault champion, Panek was one of the most decorated athletes in school history. During the mid-1920s, he earned all-state honors in football and basketball and was the leading point scorer in football every year. Panek has been inducted into the UNK Athletic Hall of Fame, Colorado Sports Hall of Fame, and Nebraska Sports Hall of Fame.

THE FULMER ERA

The 1924–1925 basketball team is notable because it had four future hall of fame members and a hall of fame coach. Clyde Cox (seated, second from left), Carl Cox (seated, fourth from left), Pat Panek (kneeling, far left), and Ihling "Brick" Carskadon (standing, far left) are members of the UNK Athletic Hall of Fame. Although the team did not win a championship (in fact, it had a losing record), it was known throughout the state as the "upsetters of dope" because it won several games based on sheer determination and will. The season opened with an out-of-state tour that saw the Antelopes drop games to the University of Wyoming and Colorado State Teachers College. Conference play opened with a promising 33-10 drubbing of Hastings College, but thereafter, with the team riddled by injury and sickness, the Antelopes dropped a string of conference games. The team, led by Panek, was especially proud of its 34-24 victory over Midland. Pictured below is Fred Fulmer Jr. with the final scoreboard.

During the mid-1920s, Clyde and Carl Cox competed for the Antelopes in football, basketball, and track. Clyde earned 12 letters during his Antelope career, the first in school history to achieve this feat. Brother Carl, who earned nine letters, was a basketball and track standout. Clyde captained the 1925 football squad, while Carl captained the 1926 track team. Both were inducted into the athletic hall of fame. From left to right are Clyde Cox, Pat Panek, Robert Huber, Carl Cox, and Allen Morris.

From left to right are members of Fred Fulmer's 1928 championship squad: (first row) Homer Boswell, Frederick "Fritz" Meyer (team captain), Marcus Morse, and Frank Dusek; (second row) Dale Kisling, Howard Boswell, and Elmer Skov; (third row) Frank Barta, coach Fred Fulmer, and James Lovell. Lovell and Dusek are members of the athletic hall of fame.

THE FULMER ERA

The winning ways of the Fulmer era disappeared during the 1930s due to a revolving door at the coaching position. The most promising coach was Randall "Wildhoss" Watkins. In three seasons, however, he failed to produce a dominant team. When Wildhoss left for the University of Wyoming in 1941, Clifton White was hired and immediately turned the program around. Pictured here is Wildhoss's 1939 basketball squad, which includes three future members of the UNK Athletic Hall of Fame: Paul Blessing, Louis Ellermeirer, and Art Stegeman.

The Antelope's second basketball championship came in 1942–1943, when the cagers topped the Nebraska Intercollegiate Athletic Association (NIAA) conference with a 10-6 record. The star that season was forward Lloyd "Mac" McCullough. Demolishing the school record for most points in a game with 42, McCullough willed his team to the school's first postseason appearance. The Antelopes lost in the first round to eventual winner Pepperdine University. Pictured at right, McCullough is boxing out his man while teammate Paul Blessing (No. 99) reaches for the rebound.

A CENTURY OF SPORTS

Pictured here is coach Fred Fulmer's 1924 track team. From left to right are (first row) Seaton Smith, Charles Rollings, John Roberts, Clyde Cox, Glenn Denton, and Ted Olson; (second row) Art Petsch, Otis Salyers, Pat Panek, and coach Fred Fulmer. Team captain Roberts dominated in the sprints and was the top point winner during the 1924 season. He set school records in the 100-, 220-, and 440-yard dashes. Other standouts were Clyde Cox, who specialized in the 880-yard run and shot put, and Pat Panek, who was an accomplished pole-vaulter.

When coach Fred Fulmer introduced cross-country as a collegiate sport in 1928, three harriers laced up the shoes for the Antelopes; from left to right are Stewart Handley, Frank Lydic, and Orlie Watts. The Antelope harriers won two Amateur Athletic Union (AAU) regional championships during Lydic's career. The 1932 team, captained and coached by Orlie Watts, was the last team fielded until coach Charlie Foster reinstated cross-country in 1956.

Possibly the greatest runner in Antelope history, Frank Lydic ran cross-country and track from 1927 to 1931. "Horse" Lydic, as he was known in his hometown of Farnam because he ran everywhere instead of riding a horse, was a member of the first cross-country team and led the harriers to winning seasons every year he competed. In track, Lydic finished his career as a four-time conference champion in the mile and two mile. In 1931, Lydic led the team to the school's first track championship by placing first in the half mile, mile, and two mile, breaking the half-mile and mile records in the process. Following his illustrious career at Kearney, Lydic reached the finals of the 1932 Olympic trials in the 1,500-meter run, falling just short of qualifying for the Olympic Games in Los Angeles. Four years later, he would go as far as the semifinals at the Olympic trials in the 5,000-meter run. As a barometer of his success, in 1931, at the AAU championships, Lydic ran a 4:15 mile, just a little over five seconds off the world record at that time. In honor of his achievements, UNK inducted Lydic into the athletic hall of fame in 1980.

For three years, Orlie Watts (middle of first row) regularly finished second to Frank Lydic. With Lydic graduated, however, Watts had a banner senior year on the cinder path. At a meet hosted by the University of Nebraska in 1932, Watts finished second in the half mile, breaking Lydic's school record. Watts competed in the 1932 Olympic trials but failed to qualify for the finals where he would have competed against his former teammate Lydic. Watts was inducted into the athletic hall of fame in 1982.

By the 1930s, the track program dominated the NIAA conference, racking up eight championships between 1930 and 1943. Originally strongest in the distance events, the program developed a dependence on its sprinters and field event athletes. The 1932 and 1933 championship teams were led by sprinters Richard Lambert, a star hurdler and sprinter, and Harold Gall, the anchor relay man and champion quarter-miler who broke the school record running a 50.9. Big man Barney Fuller (pictured here) dominated the shot put and discus.

THE FULMER ERA

Known as the "Farnam Flash," Ronald Lewis was a four-time all-conference running back and punter and a two-time conference pole vault champion. He was a surprisingly strong and swift athlete considering his unassuming build, as evidenced in this track photograph. Lewis achieved an iconic status following his performance in the 1936 football game against Peru. Scoring two touchdowns, including an 86-yard scamper, and setting up a third by intercepting a Peru pass, Lewis became something of a legend as he led the way in defeating Peru for the first time in nearly two decades. Truth be told, according to the *Antelope*, children were even named in his honor. Lewis was also the president of the K-Club during the 1937–1938 school year. Tragically, just weeks after graduating and signing a professional football contract with the Chicago Cardinals, Lewis was killed in an accident in the summer of 1938. Today, in the Farnam cemetery, one can still find the memorial that was dedicated by his fellow athletes in his honor.

The champion 1936 squad was led by a trio of weight men. Leon Swiatoviak, Barney Fuller, and Johnny Marrow finished first, second, and third in the shot put at the conference championship. From left to right are (first row) Barney Rapp, Adam Brecht, and Jerry Parker; (second row) Barney Fuller, Daniel Robbins, Art Stegeman, Charles Eisenhart, Ronald Lewis, Glen Bartunek, and John Marrow; (third row) Clark Adams, Byron Whipple, Paul Larsen, Sidney Johnson, Don Shue, Melvin Merritt, and coach Pop Klein.

The 1939 track team, led by star sprinter Melvin Rutan, was one of the strongest squads in school history. Running against large state university teams at the Colorado Relays, Rutan won the 100-yard dash and anchored the 440 relay team of Rutan, Carl Meyer, Dick Marrow, and Glen Bartunek that placed behind only Kansas State. At the conference meet Rutan took first in the 100, 220, and as the anchor of the 880 relay. As a team, the Antelopes were untouchable, racking up a record 83 team points at the conference meet—double that of second-place Peru.

THE FULMER ERA

Intercollegiate competition for women disappeared by World War I, but that does not mean that the women on campus did not compete in athletic contests. The Girl's Athletic Association (GAA) was organized in 1922. There were 62 charter members who strove to earn the 800 points required to earn a large blue and gold letter. Every Tuesday and Thursday evening, members of the GAA gathered at the gymnasium where they competed in volleyball, soccer, basketball, and swimming. Members also participated in 10-mile hikes and ice-skated on Lake Kearney.

Pop Klein introduced intercollegiate golf and tennis in the spring of 1938. In 1939, the two-man golf team of Elmer McKinney and Harold Bacon finished the year undefeated, including nonconference road wins over the University of Colorado and Fort Hays. McKinney was a force to be reckoned with on the links. During the summer of 1939, in noncollegiate events, McKinney won the Oregon Trail Golf Tournament in Scottsbluff and the Nebraska Open Championship. He also played in Chicago at the national open.

Coach Fred Fulmer's best football team was the 1922 squad. Led by a stingy defense that posted five shutouts, Fulmer's boys complied a 5-2-1 record and finished second in the league to undefeated Midland. Star players that season included Pat Panek and Rex Reed, both of whom made first-team all-state that year. After that, Fulmer's squads struggled, producing a 10-20-4 record between 1923 and 1926. By 1927, however, Fulmer put together another winning season that included a 13-10 win against Hastings College.

Hailing from tiny Stockville, brothers Rex (left) and George Reed were two of Fulmer's best football players in the early 1920s. Big, brawny farm boys, the Reed brothers were versatile and played both on the line and in the backfield. Older brother Rex played for three seasons, making first-team all-state in 1921, 1922, and 1923. The 1926 *Blue and Gold* called him "Kearney's greatest." Younger brother George followed in his footsteps and was selected to the all-state team in 1922 and 1923.

THE FULMER ERA

Going into the 1927 fray, Kearney had not beaten Hastings College since coach George Van Buren was at the helm in 1913. The 1927 game, too, looked bleak for Kearney as Hastings was inside the Antelope five-yard line with less than a minute to play. Attempting to run up the score rather than running out the clock, the Broncos were aiming for another touchdown. But following a bobbled Broncos exchange, Kearney's Ihling "Brick" Carskadon scooped up the pigskin and sprinted 97 yards for a touchdown as time expired. This 13-10 defeat of Hastings College has gone down as one of the most memorable games in school history. A multisport athlete, Carskadon was inducted into the UNK Athletic Hall of Fame in 1980.

The 1930 campaign was an exciting year for the football team. Not only did the men have a young new coach in Ted James, a former Cornhusker and professional football player, but the Antelopes were now able to host night games after the school renovated the field and added lighting. This excitement translated into a 7-0-1 record and a conference championship, the Antelopes' sole blemish coming against Hastings, who they tied 0-0 in the season finale. Pictured at left, Merle Trail, a six-foot-four-inch and 205-pound defensive standout, became the first All-America selection in school history.

The 1930 championship season produced 21 lettermen. From left to right are (first row) Ramon Pratt, Casey Merryman, Douglas Uehling, LeRoss Williams, Max Tschabrun, Darrell Noyes, Paul Jordan, and Arnold Oehlrich (assistant coach); (second row) Varley Grantham (trainer), Randall Tollefsen, Gaylord Tollefsen, Dulworth Graham, Richard Smith, Adam Brecht, Mark Malchow, and Ted James (coach); (third row) Richard Cooney, Willis Wolcott, Merle Trail (All-American), Charles Blazek, Gailord Hendrickson, Glen Beadle, Myron Hubbert, and Ivan Davis. In addition to Merle Trail, six other Antelopes were named to various all-state teams, including defensive ends Dulworth "Dode" Graham and Charlie Blazek, backfield players Randall Tollefsen and Byron Merryman, lineman LeRoss Williams, and center Paul "Pike" Jordan. Coach Ted James and four players from the 1930 team have been inducted into the UNK Athletic Hall of Fame: Merle Trail, LeRoss "Cap" Williams, Willis "Bill" Wolcott, and Dulworth "Dode" Graham.

THE FULMER ERA

During the 1930s, another set of brothers, Dode and Dud Graham, carried on the tradition of brotherly success in the blue and gold. Dulworth "Dode" Graham was an Antelope standout on the gridiron and hardwood between 1930 and 1935. As a freshman in 1930, Dode helped the Antelopes win the school's first football championship, and he earned all-conference honors in both football and basketball each of his four years. Pictured here is younger brother Dudley "Dud" Graham, who was also a standout in football and basketball.

Throughout the 1930s, the Hastings rivalry continued to escalate as the Broncos often taunted Kearney, and vice versa, by publishing comments like Hastings's 1934 proclamation that the Antelopes were "nothing but a bunch of no-account wallflowers." It seems that the rivalry reached new heights in the early 1940s, as Kearney had a number of very strong teams that pounded Hastings. To make Hastings fans even more irate, a number of Kearney fanatics "painted the Hastings campus," a feat that set off a string of campus vandalisms.

Coach Ted James resigned after posting two lackluster years in 1931 and 1932. The struggles continued under coach Howard Hill, who turned to a new pass-happy offense that in 1933 produced only nine points in eight games, earning the Antelopes their first winless campaign since 1905. After another miserable season in 1934, Fred Fulmer hired L. F. "Pop" Klein, who immediately turned the football program around with a 5-3 record during his first season. Having been a coaching legend at Crete High School, Klein came to Kearney with the remarkable career record of 89-19 in football and 200-54 in basketball. During his 10 years at Kearney, Klein led his men to three football championships and five track titles. In 1945, Klein left Kearney after accepting a football coaching position at the University of Nebraska. Klein was inducted into the UNK Athletic Hall of Fame in 1982.

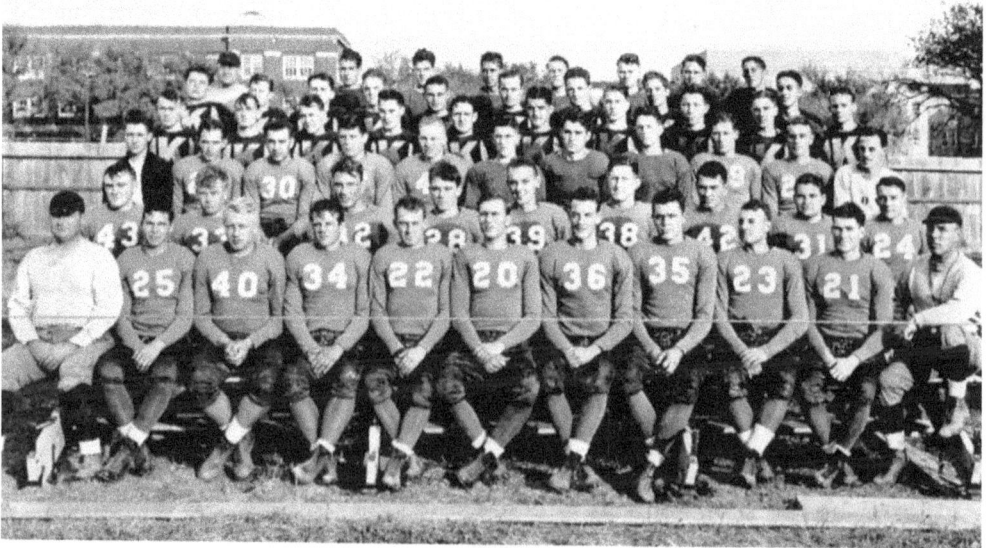

Klein's 1935 squad included future professional football player Johnny Marrow (No. 40), standouts Dud Graham (No. 31) and Byron "Barney" Fuller (No. 38), and the tandem running attack of Ronald Lewis (No. 24), and John Parilek (number unknown).

THE FULMER ERA

In these action shots from the 1938 season, the Antelopes are driving against Western Union College of Lemars, Iowa. This was the last year that this particular football field was used. The following year, with help from New Deal funding, the field was moved to where it now sits. Men's Hall can be seen under construction in the background. In the photograph above, Ben (Bennie) Taylor follows his blockers into the teeth of the Western Union defense. In the photograph below, Morrie Wilmot (No. 36) drives through a hole in the defense. The Antelopes won the game 14-0.

Three Marrow brothers—John, Marion, and Lee—have been inducted into the UNK Athletic Hall of Fame. John was an all-conference tackle in 1935 and 1936 and after graduating played professional football for the Chicago Cardinals and St. Louis Gunners. Marion was an all-conference guard and fullback during the late 1930s. Pictured here is younger brother Lee, who lettered in football, basketball, and track during the early 1940s, before his athletic career was disrupted by World War II. In 1946, he returned to campus and once again took to the field for the Antelopes.

Paul Blessing (No. 88) was a multisport athlete during his Antelope career (1938–1942). In basketball, Blessing was an all-conference sharpshooter, and in track, he gained notoriety as a discus and javelin thrower. Blessing was an even better football player. In addition to earning all-conference honors as a sophomore, junior, and senior, Blessing was an honorable mention All-American in 1941 and played for the Detroit Lions during the 1944 season. Blessing was inducted into the athletic hall of fame in 1985. Standing with Blessing are (from left to right) Bill Stafford; Carl Meyer, who was also a star on the track team and is a member of the athletic hall of fame; George Ulbrick; and Phil Shelmadine.

Because he was three to five years older than the other athletes, Art Stegeman earned the moniker "Grandad" from his younger teammates. A multisport athlete, Stegeman was known as a tough defensive player on both the football field and basketball court. When discussing Stegeman's play on the field or court, the newspapers always used words such as *stamina* and *fire*. Stegeman was inducted into the athletic hall of fame in 1980.

Going back to a power running attack, and "preaching" the importance of an impregnable defense, coach Pop Klein compiled an impressive 45-21-2 record during eight seasons. With running backs like Ronald Lewis, John Parilek, Ben Taylor, and Mike Shada, and stalwarts on the line like John Marrow, Tom Journey, Paul Blessing, and others, Klein had a burgeoning football powerhouse. When World War II broke out, the male population on campus dwindled, thinning the ranks of the football squad. Shown above, Klein is addressing his men at halftime.

Pop Klein's most powerful team was the 1941 football squad, which went undefeated and outscored its opponents 204-13. The team was led by all-conference players Paul Blessing (end), Paul Newell (guard), Tom Journey (guard), and Mike Shada (fullback). In this action shot, Shada blocks for Warren Capellan. Shada, a Kearney native, was a four-time letter winner in football (1939–1942) and in 1941 was honored as the State College Football Player of the Year by the *Lincoln Journal*. In 1982, Shada was inducted into the athletic hall of fame.

Many promising athletic careers were disrupted by World War II, and at least three members of the Antelope athletic family lost their lives. Don Johnson (pictured here), who played on the 1938 and 1939 basketball teams, joined the Army Air Corps and was killed in an accidental airplane crash on April 6, 1942. Two members of the 1941 championship football team also made the supreme sacrifice. Charles Anderson died on March 8, 1945, from wounds sustained at Iwo Jima, while Tom Erthum was killed in Italy, just weeks before the German surrender.

THE FULMER ERA

3

The Foster Era, Part I

1945–1971

For 25 years, Charlie Foster was the father of Kearney athletics. Hired in 1945 after a successful high school coaching career at Clay Center and Ansley, Foster was responsible for rebuilding the Antelope sports program after it all but disappeared during World War II. He originally served as the athletic director and the coach of all sports teams, but one by one he handed coaching duties over to new hires. In 1949, he hired Bill Morris, and later Les Livingston, to head the basketball team. In 1953, he brought in Marvin "Preacher" Franklin to head the football program, and then in 1955, he hired Allen Zikmund. Foster, according to his own attestation, decided to devote himself to track "because the teams weren't going well when I came here, so I concentrated on that sport. I began to see what I could learn about each event. I think I could have done just as well in any other sport."

Foster went on to win 20 conference championships in track and produced a number of national champions, including Clayton Scott, Merlin "Beanie" Lawrence, Hylke Van der Wal, Dennis "Duke" Dukesherer, and Jim Sobieszczyk. Foster also reintroduced cross-country in 1956 and immediately had his harriers competing for national titles. During the late 1950s and early 1960s, Foster trained All-American cross-country runners Gerald King, Larry Snell, Martin "Tuck" Mason, and dozens of others. Under Foster's guidance, the Antelope athletic program experienced a sort of golden age during the 1950s and 1960s. By the time of his retirement in 1971, six more sports were added to the athletic program, including a number of women's sports.

Wearing his familiar hat, with clipboard and stopwatch in hand, coach Charlie Foster looks toward the finish line at the now defunct track that once circled Foster Field.

In the summer of 1956, Foster took seven athletes on a cross-country road trip to participate in the Olympic trials in California. Although they came up short, it was a memorable trip for all. Pictured above are Foster and four of the seven athletes. From left to right are Joe McFarland, a broad jump specialist; Foster (behind the wheel); Don Ayers, the conference champion in the 100 and 220; Jim Hansen, a talented shot put and discus thrower; and Clayton Scott, Kearney's two-time national champion in the two mile.

During the Foster era, distance runners consistently led the always-dominant Antelope track team. This began in 1954 with Clayton Scott's national championship in the two mile. The Grand Island native went on to break Orlie Watt's 880 record and reestablished his own two-mile record by running a 9:28.4 when he repeated as the national champion. Pictured at right are Scott and Foster, with his trusty stopwatch in hand. Scott was inducted into the UNK Athletic Hall of Fame in 1995.

Larry Snell was one of Foster's best all-around runners. A cross-country and track star, Snell was the first runner ever to win the Omaha World Herald Nebraska College Athlete of the Year award. He won All-America honors in the mile and the 1,500- and 5,000-meter runs. As a junior, Snell ran a 4:14.7 mile, breaking Lydic's 30-year-old record. His best time in the 1,500-meter run was a 3:52.7, a time that nearly half a century later still stands as the second best in school history. Snell was inducted into the UNK Athletic Hall of Fame in 1993.

Martin "Tuck" Mason was Charlie Foster's finest middle-distance runner and arguably the best half-miler in school history. In 1962, Mason sprinted to a time of 1:50.29 in the 800-meter run, a time that stood as the school record until 2001, when Joe Cooper ran six-tenths of a second better. Mason finished his career as an All-American in both cross-country and track. He was inducted into the UNK Athletic Hall of Fame in 1981. Above, Mason is leading the pack at the "naval battle" with Wayne. Despite the waterlogged track, Mason still ran the 880 in 2:02.

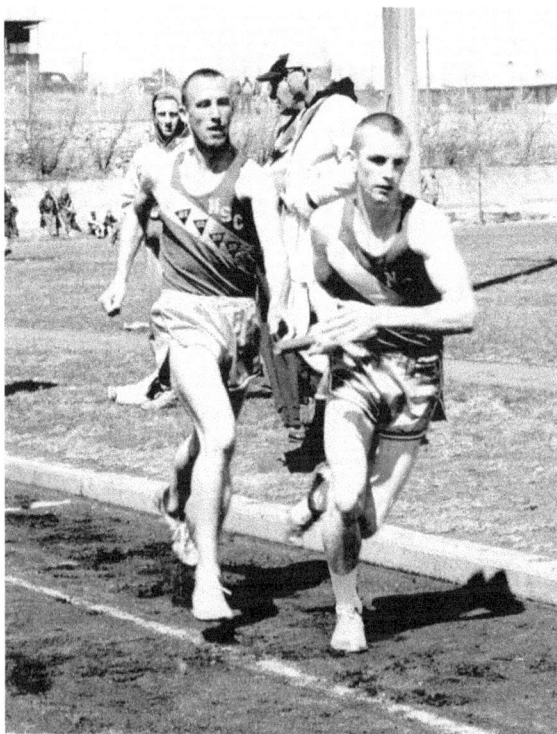

Foster produced a number of dominant steeplechasers, including five All-Americans. One of them was Gary Shubert, who ran track and cross-country during the late 1950s and early 1960s (other All-American steeplechasers include Ray Mars, Hylke Van der Wal, Jim Scherzberg, and Don Peterson). Shubert earned All-America honors in the steeplechase in 1960, while in 1961, his eighth-place finish at the national meet earned him All-America status in cross-country. In this photograph, Shubert hands off the baton to Larry Moore. Shubert was inducted into the UNK Athletic Hall of Fame in 2007.

Hylke Van der Wal was the most versatile runner in school history. Coming to Kearney from Canada, after being born in the Netherlands, Van der Wal still holds top-10 times in school history in the 800-meter run (1:53), 1,500-meter run (3:52.9), the 3,000-meter steeplechase (9:00.2), the mile (4:10.04), and the 1,000-yard run (2:10.4). Van der Wal was a two-time All-American in the steeplechase and the 1961 National Association of Intercollegiate Athletics (NAIA) national champion. He was inducted into the UNK Athletic Hall of Fame in 2006.

Warren Christensen was a dominant distance runner during the late 1960s. Pictured above, onlookers watch Christensen sprint toward the line during the final leg of the two-mile relay. Besides anchoring several relay teams, Christensen was also a talented runner in the opens. For example, he owns the school's best time in the mile—a 4:07.8—and has a top-10 time in the 1,500-meter run.

As is evidenced by the photograph above, track meets produced standing-room-only crowds in the 1940s. Bob Hauver was one of the finest track athletes during the 1940s. Above, he is pictured (fourth from left) competing in the 100-yard dash at the now defunct track that once circled Foster Field. Hauver returned to his alma mater as a multisport coach and took over the track program in 1972. Pictured at left is 440 master Harvey Stroud. In 1949, he broke the conference and school record by running a 50.8. Stroud and Hauver also excelled on the football field.

THE FOSTER ERA, PART I

Don Straney (pictured at right), an All-American in 1954, was one of the fastest sprinters of the Foster era. He was one of the first Antelope runners to run under 50 seconds in the quarter mile. Straney teamed with Don Ayers, Bob Miller, and Milt Johnson to form one of the best relay teams in school history. Their 1:28.5 880-yard relay time was the fourth-fastest time in the United States in 1956. Thanks to that time, the team qualified to compete in the Olympic trials. Pictured below are two members of that record-setting relay: Milt Johnson (far right) and Don Ayers (second from right). When he graduated in 1956, Ayers held 14 conference track meet records. Ayers was inducted into the UNK Athletic Hall of Fame in 1999.

Pictured here is early shot put standout Eugene "Bulldog" Turner, who held the conference shot put record in 1954. Turner was also an animal on the football field, earning all-conference honors as a center his senior year. An all-around athlete who was inducted into the UNK Athletic Hall of Fame in 1983, Turner earned four letters in track, four in football, and two in basketball.

Seen here is Francis Hircock, an eccentric big man who dominated the shot put between 1958 and 1961. He earned All-America honors in 1958, 1960, and 1961. His best put was 55 feet and 1 inch, a distance that, as of 2007, is still number five on the school's all-time outdoor top-10 marks.

During the 1950s, coach Charlie Foster produced many champion shot putters. Four of those athletes earned All-America honors. Jim Jacobs (right), whose best put was 54 feet and 6.5 inches, earned All-America honors in the shot put and discus. Below is the 1965 honorable mention All-American tandem of Jim Owens (left) and Randy Rasmussen (right).

In addition to his strong shot putters, Charlie Foster also produced four All-American discus men. Doyle Fyfe, shown at left, was a three-sport athlete who won 12 athletic letters. He was an All-American discus thrower in 1955.

LeRoy Sprague, pictured here in his practice gear, was named an All-American in 1958 after finishing in fourth place at the national meet. Jim Jacobs complemented his shot put performance and was named an All-American in discus in 1958. The best discus man of the Foster era was All-American Charlie Hircock, who flung the discus 158 feet and 8.5 inches.

In 1964 and 1965, some of the school's best long jump marks were set by a trio of jumpers: Bob Whitehouse, Jim Schaefer, and Jerry Stuckert. Whitehouse, a four-time All-American (1962–1965), owns the school's all-time second-best jump at 24 feet and 2.5 inches. In 1965, Schaefer went 24 feet and 2 inches but did not place at the national meet. Another jumper to go over 24 feet was Jerry Stuckert (pictured here), who was an All-American in 1963.

Pictured here is Kearney's javelin ace, Gary Mason. In 1963, Mason threw the javelin 223 feet and 9 inches, a mark that stands as the farthest in school history. He was named an All-American in 1961. High jump king Jim Sobieszczyk was also outstanding. In 1970, he tossed the javelin 208 feet and 9 inches. Terry Reike, Augie Nelson, and Chuck Bolton were also talented javelin throwers.

Coach Charlie Foster produced a slew of All-American pole-vaulters. Dale Falter was the first, earning the honor in 1956. Merlin "Beanie" Lawrence (pictured here) consistently cleared 14 feet and was the NAIA national pole vault champion in 1960. He finished his career as a three-time All-American (1959–1961) and was inducted into the UNK Athletic Hall of Fame in 1992. Fred Williams was the next great vaulter and was an All-American in 1963 and 1965. Along with Williams, Jack Ehler, Dennis "Duke" Dukesherer, and Steve Welch were also named All-Americans during the Foster era.

Dennis "Duke" Dukesherer, as he was called, went on to become a four-time All-American and the 1967 NAIA national pole vault champion. His vault of 15 feet and 7.5 inches stood as the school record for 12 years. Besides his outstanding work in the vault, Duke was also a very talented jumper and hurdler. In 1969, he was the Nebraska College Conference (NCC) champion in the long jump (23 feet and 7.5 inches, fifth-best in school history) and triple jump (46 feet and 6.25 inches).

THE FOSTER ERA, PART I

High jumpers must have had fortitude during the early Foster era. In this photograph, Lynn Porter stands in front of the high jump pit filled with sawdust. Foster's best high jumpers were Dennis McGraw and Jim Sobieszczyk. In 1965, at the NCC conference meet, McGraw raised the school record to six feet and eight inches, a height that stills puts him among the top jumpers in school history.

Jim Sobieszczyk (pictured here) was the first Nebraskan to high jump seven feet. Sobieszczyk was the NAIA national champion in 1970 and the indoor champ in 1971. His winning jump of seven feet still stands as the school record some three decades later. After graduating, Sobieszczyk went on to become one the of nation's best decathlon athletes. He qualified for the Olympic trials in the decathlon in 1972, 1976, 1980, and 1984. Sobieszczyk was inducted into the UNK Athletic Hall of Fame in 1990.

Photographed above are the members of the 1967 mile relay team. From left to right are Roger Nielsen, Jim Jensen, Ron Brewer, and John Eckhout. The next season Jensen, Brewer, and Eckhout, along with Nate Butler, went on to run a 3:12.7, a time that still stands as the best in school history. Butler ran on a number of record-breaking relay teams, including the 1970 national champion two-mile relay team. Other members of those teams were Tim Enck, Wayne Phipps, Al Rasmussen, and Rich Molczyk. Another record-holding relay team was the distance medley team of Ed Kester, Daryl Broberg, Tuck Mason, and Hylke Van der Wal, who are pictured below from left to right. The "Lightning Lopers," as they were called, still hold the school record in the distance medley.

Larry Sallinger, who ran for Charlie Foster in the mid-1960s, was arguably the greatest hurdler in school history. Shown above, Sallinger is displaying his envious form. Perhaps the most underrated track star during Foster's era, Sallinger has the best time in school history in the 110 highs, with a 14.4, and the 55-meter hurdles, which he ran in just under 7.3 seconds. On top of his work in the hurdle races, Sallinger also ran on a number of relay teams, including the 880 relay team that holds the second-best time in school history.

Athletes who earned four letters in a single sport were awarded a "K-Blanket." Pictured here are those who earned blankets in 1962. From left to right are (first row) Vince Bramer, Doug Marcy, Gary Shubert, and Tuck Mason; (second row) Larry Dieckman, Merlin "Beanie" Lawrence, Ken Kuhn, Jerry Liveringhouse, and Daryl Broberg.

Wrestling was introduced as an intercollegiate sport during the 1960–1961 school year. Pictured above is the 1965 wrestling squad. Standing seventh from the left is Sen. Chuck Hagel, who had a brief Antelope athletic career before joining the military. During this period, the Antelope wrestlers were coached by Bob Hauver, Joe Willis, and Jack Ramey. Pictured at left is Don Hather, an exceptional heavyweight wrestler who led his team to a NCC championship in 1963. During his junior and senior seasons, in 1963 and 1964, Hather's only losses came at the NAIA national meet, where he placed eighth and fifth, respectively. Hather was inducted into the UNK Athletic Hall of Fame in 1995.

Pictured here is Warren "Mike" Monnington, a three-sport athlete in the late 1940s and early 1950s. During his athletic career, Monnington earned 11 letters, including four in basketball, four in track, and three in football. He was a team leader during the 1948–1949 basketball season and earned all-state honors. Monnington was inducted into the UNK Athletic Hall of Fame in 1989.

Coached by Charlie Foster, the 1947–1948 squad finished with a respectable 11-5 record due in large part to the scoring abilities of Bob Korte, the first great player of the period. A two-time all-state forward, Korte averaged 23 points per game and scored 465 points in 1948–1949, a record at the time. The 1949 basketball team, pictured above, had a number of UNK Athletic Hall of Fame athletes. Seated in the front are Bob Hauver (No. 88), Warren Monnington (No. 33), and Bob Korte (No. 44). Doyle Fitzke (No. 12) is standing in the center of the back row.

During the Foster era, the basketball program produced no conference championships and only a handful of winning seasons. The hiring of Les Livingston in 1956 gave some life to a struggling program. His 1957–1958 team, for example, produced a 14-7 record but lost in the first round of the playoffs. Pictured above are members of that team. From left to right are (first row) Leo Fleming, Noel Olin, Wayne Casper, Gary Smidt, Gene Lawhead, Bill Beavers, Tom Williams, Nelson Hinkle, and George Haun; (second row) Dick Wiegand, Gene Armstrong, LeRoy Sprague, Paul Collison, Jim Jacobs, Jim Hanson, and coach Les Livingston. Notable players include UNK Athletic Hall of Fame members Armstrong, Collison, Smidt, and Sprague. Pictured below are cocaptains LeRoy Sprague (left) and Dick Wiegand, who are posing with their pen sets, traditionally given to team captains.

During the late 1950s, Gary Smidt rewrote the Kearney records books. In his junior year, Smidt led his team and the conference in scoring, finishing the season averaging 17.6 points per game. During the same season, he also led the NCC in free throw percentage, shooting 81 percent from the charity stripe. The next season, Smidt went on to break nearly all the single-season scoring marks, as he scored 505 points for the season and averaged more than 22 points a game. Pictured at right, Smidt is scoring over Hastings's star player, and future Cornhusker football coach, Tom Osborne. Below, Smidt shoots from the outside.

"Tall Paul" Collison, as he answered to, was the "Rebound King" and one of the best centers in school history. Collison holds a number of season and career rebounding records. For example, in a 1957 game against Colorado School of Mines, Collison set a game record by grabbing 32 rebounds. With 1,271 career rebounds, Collison sits number one on the all-time list. In this photograph, Collison soars down the lane for two points in a 1959 game against Dana College.

As the picture above reveals, seating was limited in the old gymnasium to a few rows courtside, with additional seating overlooking the court on the third floor. The aging gymnasium could not accommodate the growing athletic programs. Locker space was limited, and the hardwood court did not meet collegiate size requirements, forcing the basketball team to play its home games at local high school gymnasiums. With the completion of Cushing Coliseum in 1961, the basketball team once again began playing home games on campus.

Baseball officially returned to Kearney in 1961 under the supervision of coach Bill Giles. In 1963, the team won its first NCC championship behind the slugging of Ronald Anderson, who finished the season with a .414 percent batting average. In 1966, the program began its streak of three consecutive titles under the guidance of coach Fred Gerhardt. The 1967 team was selected to play in the NAIA national tournament. After Gerhardt tragically died of a heart attack in the summer of 1968, Jerry Hueser was named coach for the 1969 season.

Rich Osentowski led the Loper baseball squads during the late 1960s with his hitting prowess. Osentowski, who was also a star quarterback, batted .475 in 1967, the highest batting average in school history. Osentowski finished his career as a three-time All-American and was drafted by the Minnesota Twins. Other standout players of the 1960s were pitchers Don Wilson and Del Prindle, whose 0.48 and 0.66 ERAs still rank first and second on the all-time list.

Intercollegiate sports for women disappeared prior to World War I. By the 1960s, however, as the baby boom generation reached adulthood and a wave of liberation swept the nation, athletic opportunities for women began to appear. The first chance for competition came in the swimming pool. The women's swimming program was founded by coach Harriet Yingling in 1962, but by the late 1960s, Joan Bailey headed the swim team, a position she held for 29 years. Pictured from left to right are national swimming qualifiers Nita Lechner, Peg Harrington, Su Jacob, Cindy Hauver, and Janis Watson.

In addition to swimming, by the late 1960s, softball, volleyball, and basketball emerged as intercollegiate sports for women. Softball was introduced in 1966 under the leadership of coach Joan Bailey, and volleyball was introduced in 1968 by Rosella Meier. Women's basketball was reinstated in 1967–1968, and coach Connie Hansen yielded a squad of 18 women.

Golf, like the rest of the sports at Kearney, made a comeback after World War II. After being coached by Charlie Foster for two seasons, the team was then coached by Bill Morris between 1948 and 1955, and Les Livingston between 1956 and 1981. Pictured here is Jim Tschepl, the most capable golfer of the era. At the NAIA national meet, Tschepl finished 18th in 1967 and 21st in 1968.

Tennis was brought back as an intercollegiate sport in the spring of 1947. Marge Elliot coached the team for three seasons before being succeeded by Bill Morris. In 1957, Les Livingston took over and guided the program to its first NCC championship in 1959. The program then went on to win NCC titles in 1961–1964, 1967, and 1969, when they went undefeated. The superb players of the era were Larry Marshall, Gary Smidt, W. "Rocky" Ford, Doug Grundy, Jerry Anderson, John Richman, Ron Hofmann, Bob Lapp, Dennis Fisher, Les Livingston Jr., and Greg Cheng.

Despite the incredible dominance of the football team and the success of the track program, Kearney's first team national championship did not come on the football field or cinder track. Instead the first national honor came at the bowling lanes. Pictured here is the 1964 bowling team that won the NAIA national championship. From left to right are Bob Lapp, Dave Sparks, Denny Renter, John Headrick, and By Blobaum. The Antelope bowlers were led by John Headrick, who won the individual national title that year.

Leland Copeland joined the athletic department as an assistant coach in 1946. His greatest contribution was his devotion to building a strong intramural program. To honor his long and significant contribution to Kearney athletics, the renovated gymnasium was renamed Copeland Hall. Today the Leland and Jean Copeland Intramural Award is awarded to the male and female who best represent the qualities admired by Copeland: fair play, loyalty, broad athletic talent, and sportsmanship. Pictured here is Copeland presenting the 1960 Intramural MVP Award to Gary Kruse (left) and Jim Krueger.

Charlie Foster reinstated cross-country in 1956, and for 12 consecutive seasons, his harriers captured the NCC championship. Foster's distance runners also finished in the top 10 in the nation eight times between 1956 and 1965. Pictured here from left to right are four members of Foster's first cross-country team: Ray Mars, Larry Snell, Dale Harsen, and Jerry King. Snell and King earned All-America honors in 1956. Other all-Americans during the Foster era include Gary Schubert (1959 and 1961), Ray Mars (1959), Phil Dean (1960), Tuck Mason (1960), Don Peterson (1962 and 1963), and Clarence Wiedel (1963).

The 1959 District 11 NAIA and Midwest AAU meet was held in Omaha on a bitterly cold day. With temperatures as low as 14 degrees, the Antelopes finished in first place, ahead of the University of Nebraska. Pictured here are Foster and race winner Larry Snell as he nears the finish line.

Charlie Foster's most successful year was 1959 when his distance boys finished just four points shy of champion Emporia State at the national meet. Pictured above are members of the 1959 team. From left to right are (kneeling) Ray Mars and Larry Moore; (standing) coach Bob Hauver, Dale Harsen, Gary Shubert, Larry Snell, Phil Dean, Tuck Mason, and coach Charlie Foster. Pictured at left is 1959 All-American Ray Mars.

Despite losing All-Americans Phil Dean (right), Tuck Mason, and Gary Shubert to graduation, the 1962 cross-country team remained strong, finishing fourth in the nation. Pictured below are standouts from that season. From left to right are Clarence Wiedel, Don Peterson, and Al Schneider. Peterson earned All-America honors in 1962 and 1963, while Clarence Wiedel was awarded honorable mention status in 1963.

In 1971, Charlie Foster was forced to retire due to a mandatory retirement age requirement. About his retirement, Foster once said, "Frankly this retirement business is a lot of malarkey—telling somebody they can't do something because they're that old," a statement that suggests that his fire was far from extinguished. Foster did not stay away from coaching for long. After retiring, he founded the women's track program, and in 1976, he added women's cross-country. Foster was inducted into the Helms Foundation Hall of Fame in track and field in 1960 and the NAIA Hall of Fame in 1968. He was also the first inductee into the UNK Athletic Hall of Fame. In this photograph, Foster solemnly accepts one of his 20 NCC track titles while coach Allen Zikmund offers a helping hand.

4

THE FOSTER ERA, PART II

1945–1971

During the Foster era, three different coaches guided the football program. Charlie Foster coached the Antelopes from 1945 to 1952, earning an impressive 42-24-3 record. He coached some of the Antelope greats on the gridiron, including Bob Hauver, Cecil Patterson, Paul Marzolf, Dick Elm, and Eddie Staab. In 1953, Foster began focusing on the development of what would become a track dynasty and thus hired Marvin "Preacher" Franklin to take over the football program. A standout collegiate player at Vanderbilt, Franklin guided the Antelopes for only two seasons before leaving for Houston, Texas.

The hiring of Allen Zikmund, a former Cornhusker and accomplished high school coach, lifted the Blue and Gold football program to new heights. In 17 seasons, Zikmund won 11 conference championships and coached a number of All-Americans, including Merlin Bachman, Mike Augustyn, Claire Boroff, Larry Jacobsen, Dick Butloph, Lee Jacobsen, Ed Kruml, and John Makovicka. Although the winning tradition would continue after Zikmund's retirement, his years at the helm were truly the golden age of Blue and Gold football.

When football returned to full strength in 1945, coach Charlie Foster led his gridiron men to a 5-1 record. This was the most successful season under his leadership, which ended following the 1952 season. Above are some of the key members of the first post–World War II football team. Taking instructions from Foster are, from left to right, Cecil Patterson, Ken Shibata, Wallace Walker, and Francis Bell. Patterson was the team's best player during his two seasons at Kearney. In fact, Patterson was such a prolific runner that he was known as "the one man offense." During his time in the backfield, Patterson helped lead the Antelopes to an 11-3-1 record. In the photograph below, the Antelopes plunge across the goal line for a touchdown.

Pictured here are two action shots from Foster's post–World War II football teams. In the photograph above, Max Osborne is hauling down a Wesleyan rusher while teammate Hal Spohn comes to his aid. In the photograph below, legendary Antelope Bob Hauver carries the ball. Note the limited padding and helmet gear worn by these Antelope football players.

Standing in the north end zone are members of the 1950 football team. Unfortunately, this squad owns the dubious distinction of suffering the first loss to Hastings during the Foster era. After four straight wins, and a tie in 1949, the all-time record with Hastings stood at 12-15-5, in Hastings's favor. However, despite the early wins of the period, Hastings then went on to win the next three, including a blowout in 1952. Under coach Marvin "Preacher" Franklin, the teams split their games with their archrival.

Warren "Mike" Monnington was a three-sport athlete. On the gridiron, Monnington played on both the offense and defense. He played on Charlie Foster's 1947 team that beat Roswell New Mexico Air Force Base by a score of 27-13 in the Antelopes' first-ever postseason game.

Pictured at right, in his two-point stance, is Kearney native Dick Elm. As the captain of the 1952 football team, Elm was known for his determination and surprising speed. From his fullback position, Elm led the team in rushing. Below is quarterback Eddie Staab, who was the other offensive star during the early 1950s. Besides being a talented baseball player who played for a New York Yankees farm league team, Staab was the best throwing quarterback of the 1950s. Two of his favorite receivers were ends Herman Hinkle, the oldest of the many Hinkle brothers who played in the blue and gold, and Paul Marzolf.

Pictured here are coach Marvin "Preacher" Franklin and all-conference center and team captain Eugene "Bulldog" Turner. Franklin, who played football at Vanderbilt University and later graduated from Yale Divinity School, took over for coach Charlie Foster in 1953. In his two seasons at Kearney, Franklin led his teams to an 8-8-2 record. Remembered by those who knew him as having the most dynamic coaching personality of anyone in school history, it was not a surprise when he decided to leave Kearney for greener pastures in Houston, Texas.

Four-year letterman Doyle Fyfe was a mainstay on the Kearney line between 1951 and 1954 and one of the great all-around athletes in school history. During his four years at Kearney, he earned 12 letters (four each in football, basketball, and track). After a successful high school coaching career, Fyfe returned to his alma mater, serving as assistant basketball coach for 10 years. Fyfe was inducted into the UNK Athletic Hall of Fame in 1980.

In 1955, the football program was given a shot in the arm when Allen Zikmund, a former Cornhusker football star, was hired to coach the football team. In his first season, Zikmund led the Antelopes to their first NCC conference championship. Winning championships soon became commonplace, as Zikmund's football team took home 11 championships in 17 campaigns. Pictured below, Zikmund's Antelopes gather around for a pregame pep talk.

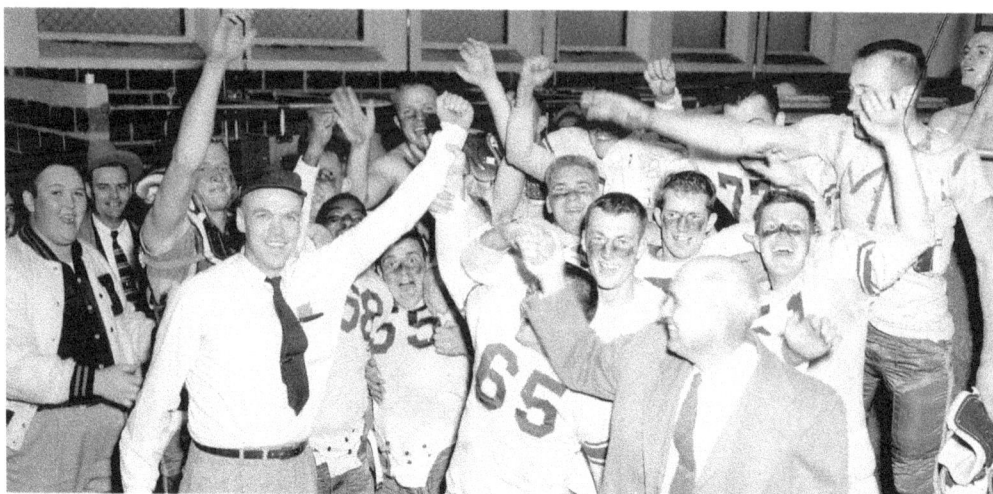

Pictured above is the 1955 football team celebrating the school's first-ever NCC conference championship, which it wrapped up after defeating Midland Lutheran College. Included in the photograph are coach Allen Zikmund (left foreground) and offensive standouts Dave Brink and Ray Adams, who are directly behind Zikmund. Also in the photograph are Charlie Foster (right foreground) and defensive stalwart Mike Augustyn, as they share a congratulatory handshake. Pictured below, members of the 1955 squad admire their championship trophy with Zikmund. After winning a NCC championship, the Antelopes beat Northern State in the Botany Bowl.

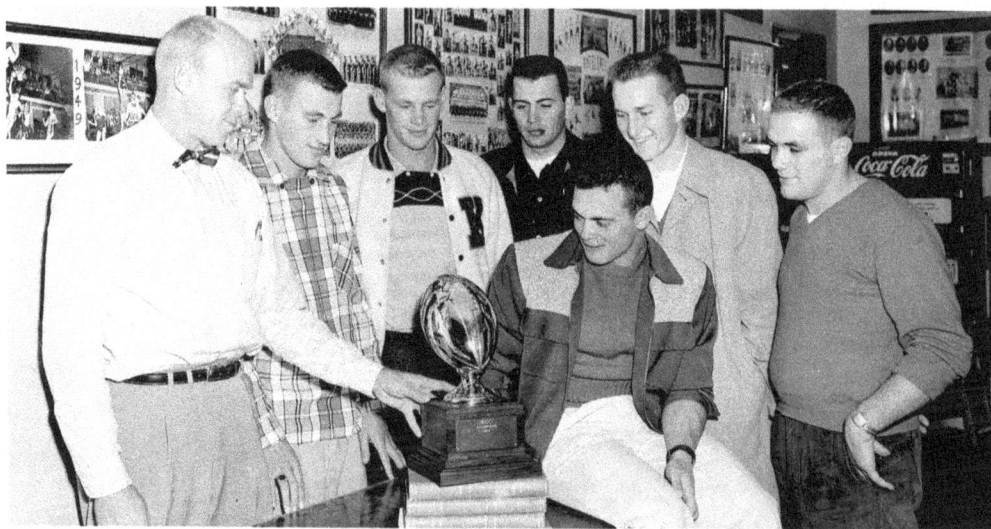

Ray Adams was the first outstanding African American athlete in school history. At Blythe Junior College in California, Adams was a two-time All-American. Adams transferred to Kearney in 1954 and immediately made an impact on the gridiron. In his first season, he averaged nearly six yards per carry and led the team in rushing. As a senior and cocaptain, the all-conference running back was the best offensive player on the talent-laden 1955 football squad that won the NCC championship and the school's first-ever bowl game win. Pictured below, Adams springs through a hole created by a ferocious Jim Patsios block (No. 35).

Merlin Bachman was a cocaptain on the 1955 squad. During his Antelope football career, the rugged Bachman played every position but center. An outstanding receiver, grinding runner, and "tougher than nails" linebacker, Bachman was named an All-American in 1955 and was inducted into the UNK Athletic Hall of Fame in 1989.

Above are teammates Dave Brink and Mike Augustyn. Brink was a three-time all-conference selection at tight end. On top of his exceptional pass-catching abilities, Brink, who is standing at left, was also a talented defensive player and a weight man on Charlie Foster's track teams. The team's defensive star and most exceptional lineman was Mike Augustyn, who was named a second-team All-American in 1956 and an All-American and recipient of the Carriker Award for the state's most outstanding lineman in 1957.

The talent-filled 1958 football team finished the season 9-0 and outscored opponents 389-42. Posing here is the 1958 starting offense. On the line, from left to right, are Charlie Thorell, Bob Clay, Garey Yocum, Bill Welte, Jerry Ball, Marvin Schleeman, and Gary Welton. The backfield includes, from left to right, Gary Smidt, Gene Lawhead, Larry Jacobsen, and Claire Boroff. Thorell, Welte, Jacobsen, and Boroff earned all-conference honors in 1958.

The 1958 defense posted four shutouts and surrendered only 42 points against nine opponents. The rushing defense was exceptional, giving up only 763 rushing yards. From left to right are (kneeling) Don Wisch, Ollie Goa, Doug Marcy, Dick O'Neil, Chuck Bolton, and Jim Jacobs; (standing) Wes Mosher, Gary Smidt, Bill Welte, Larry Jacobsen, and Gary Johnson. .

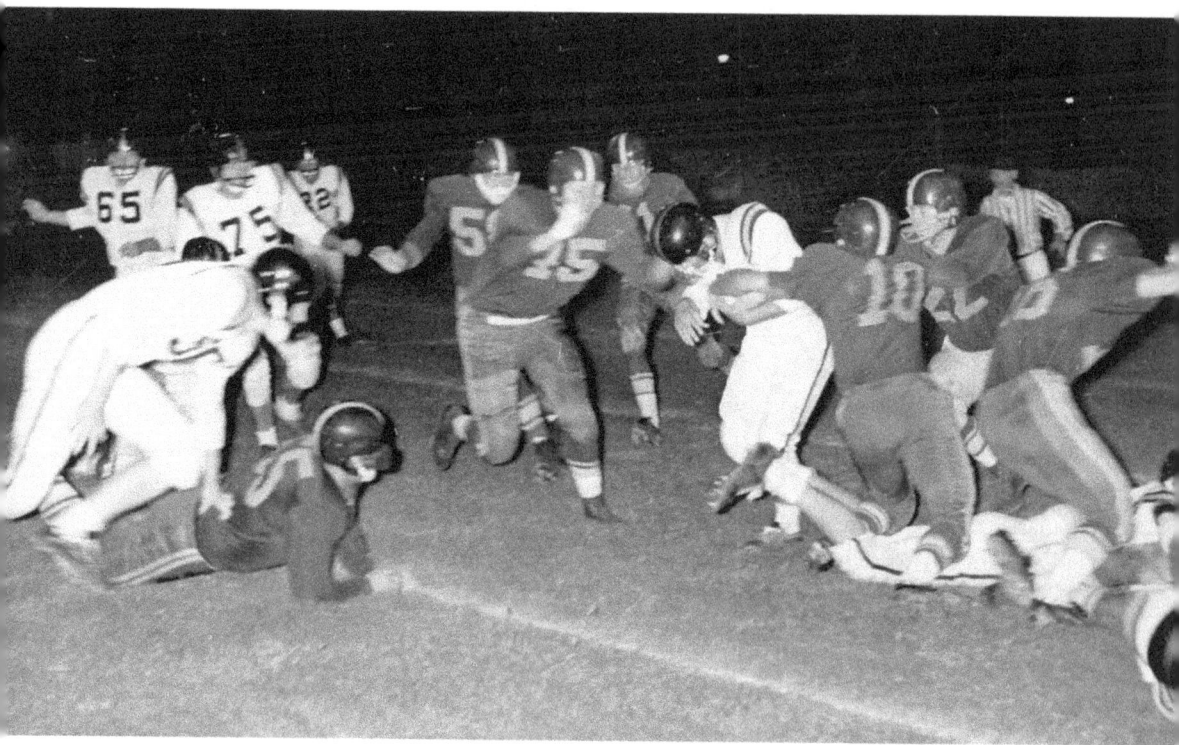

Oftentimes lost in all the offensive accolades were Allen Zikmund's outstanding defenses. For example, in 1957, the Antelope defense held Midland Lutheran College to just 21 yards of total offense—a statistic that remains the school record. Other impressive statistics were accomplished in 1959 when Midland Lutheran was held to −31 yards rushing. In terms of pass defense, Zikmund's teams were also strong. During Zikmund's stint, eight times his defense held the opponents to less than 20 yards passing. And in terms of total defense, seven times his defenses held their opponents to less than 100 yards of offense. What makes these numbers so impressive is that many of the defensive stars played both sides of the ball. Larry Jacobsen, for example, is second for career rushing yards but earned All-America status as a defensive player. In this photograph, defensive stalwarts Jim Jacobs (No. 45), Larry Jacobsen (No. 10), and Bill Welte (No. 22) converge on an opposing back.

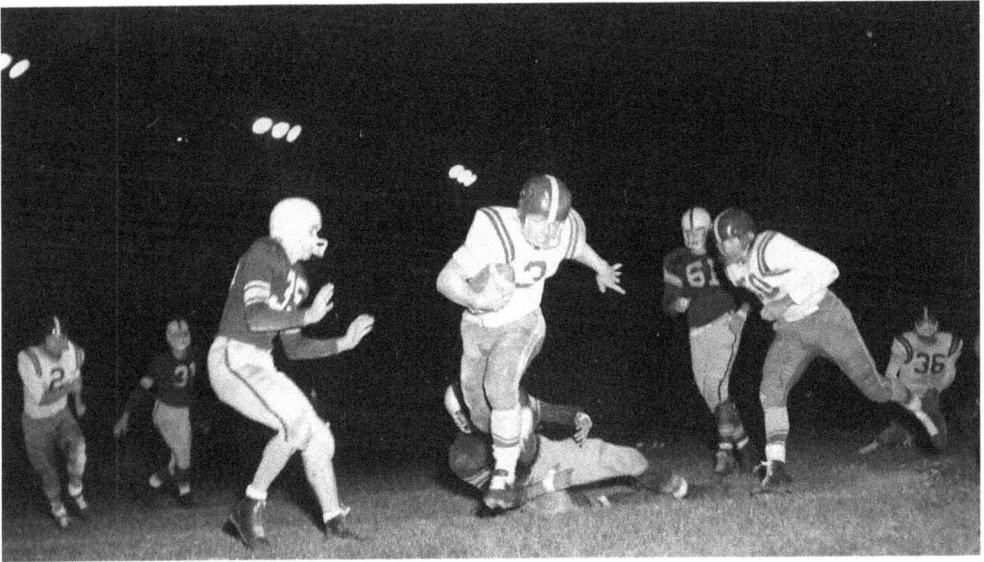

In 1957 and 1958, Claire Boroff led the NCC in scoring. One of his most outstanding performances came against Dana College in 1958 when he had touchdown runs of 97 yards (still the longest in school history), 57 yards, and 16 yards, not to mention his 61-yard reception for a touchdown. The first-team All-American from Grand Island was also a dependable kicker. In 1958, he was 35-40 on extra-point tries. Boroff was inducted into the UNK Athletic Hall of Fame in 1987.

Boroff's backfield running partner, Larry Jacobsen, was one of the most prolific ball carriers in Antelope history. In 1959, he led the entire NAIA in rushing and was named an NAIA All-American. Jacobsen, who was known as the "Homer Thunderbolt," stills holds the school's record for career yards per carry, at better than seven yards per attempt, and is ranked second in career rushing with 2,982 yards. Jacobsen was inducted into the UNK Athletic Hall of Fame in 1985.

In 1957, the Antelopes entered the Hastings game with a 15-game winning streak. Led by quarterback Tom Osborne, the Broncos jumped out to a 26-0 halftime lead and went on to win 26-7, snapping the Antelope's longest winning streak in school history. Although Kearney finished the season 8-1, the loss to Hastings denied the Antelopes a third straight NCC championship. Tom Osborne recalled that Hastings's victory was "the most memorable game of my playing career." In the photograph above of the 1960 Hastings contest, Jerry Dunlap (No. 12) carries the ball while Steve Kraus (No. 15) and Gary Meyers (No. 41) clear the path. Kearney won the game by a score of 25-12.

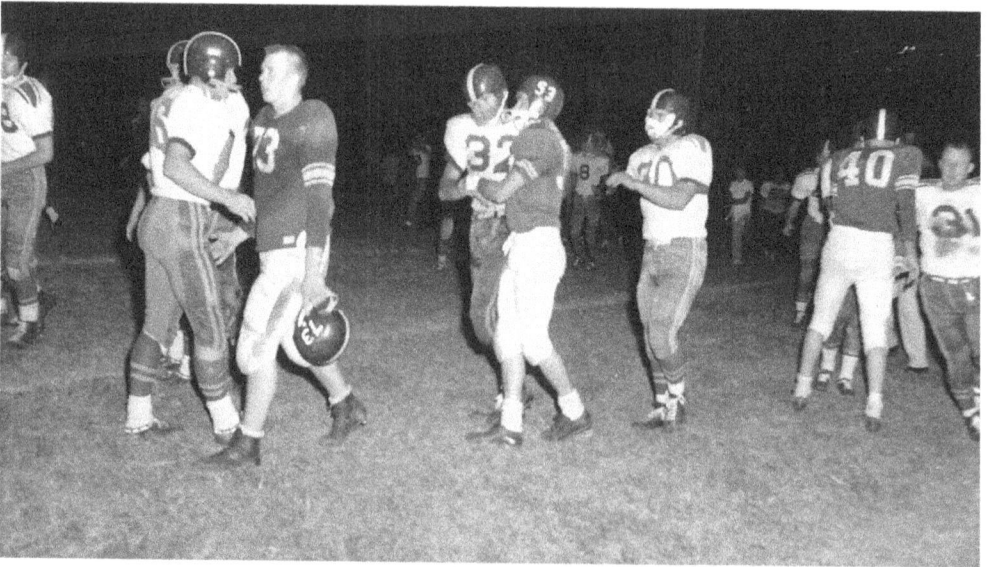

Fans from Kearney and Hastings helped fuel the fire of rivalry. In 1958, for example, the Hastings fans burned a large H on the Antelopes' football field, while Kearney fans retaliated the following year by tearing down both goal posts at Hastings after the Antelopes won 26-7. While the fans may have been involved in mischief, at the end of the game players always displayed sportsmanship with a congratulatory handshake, as the photograph above suggests.

THE FOSTER ERA, PART II

The rivalry with Hastings became so intense that during the 1950s a new tradition arrived on campus: Bronco Days. During the week leading up to the Hastings-Kearney football game, the student body hyped themselves by engaging in a number of activities. For example, in 1958, students constructed a dilapidated old shanty with a sign on it reading, "Welcome to Hastings College." During the week a burro also graced the front lawn of the student union. As well, there was a campus contest for the best-dressed cowgirl and cowboy, the best-dressed cowboy faculty member, and the best-bearded man. During the weekly festivities, a campus picnic was held where students often chanted sayings like "What'll we eat? . . . Bronco Meat!" The night before the game was the big bonfire and pep rally. Pictured above is Don Welch, as he leads the stubborn burro ridden by Doc Jeldon.

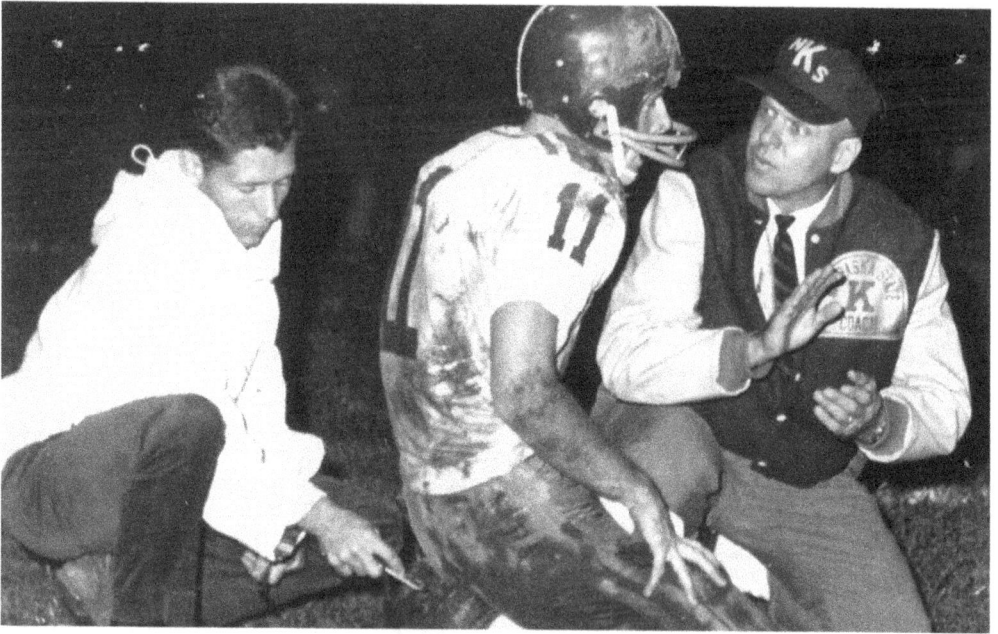

In this photograph, a beat-up Dick Butolph receives instructions from coach Allen Zikmund while team manager Jerry Steele scrapes mud from the quarterback's cleats. On the very next play, Butolph led the Antelopes to a touchdown against Fort Hays.

Bill Backes (No. 4) was a regular in the Antelope backfield in the early 1960s. He played an important role in the 1963 offensive machine that played in the NAIA playoffs and was ranked as high as No. 3 in the nation. In the game against Northern State that season, Backes scored four touchdowns, a feat that has been done only eight times since the 1950s.

Quarterback Dick Butolph (left) and receiver Jim Irwin were one of the most prolific tandems in school history. In 1963, against Wayne State, Butolph passed for five touchdowns, including three touchdown passes of 71, 62, and 43 yards to Irwin. Irwin was drafted by the Los Angeles Rams while Butolph was selected by the Ottawa Roughriders of the Canadian league. Both Butoloph and Irwin are members of the UNK Athletic Hall of Fame.

The 1963 football team was one of the strongest squads in school history. Led by a stifling defense and an offensive machine that included Dick Butolph and Jim Irwin, Kearney's All-American quarterback and receiver, the team finished the regular season undefeated and ranked third in the nation. Pictured above are the 1963 seniors. From left to right are (first row) Don Hather, Howard Hanson, Jim Irwin, Dick Butoloph, and Sterling Troxel; (second row) Terry Renner, Dick Hollinger, Jim Ekerberg, Charlie Hircock, and John Johnson.

As a result of the Antelopes' successful regular season, Kearney hosted an NAIA playoff game against Prairie View A&M. The game was played in the bitter cold with windchill as low as 20 degrees below zero, as the wardrobe in the photograph above indicates. (Standing from left to right are an unnamed NAIA official, coach Charlie Foster, Gov. Frank B. Morrison, and coach Allen Zikmund.) Although the Antelopes led 7-0 at the half, late in the game the team committed two costly errors, a blocked punt inside its own five-yard line and a Butolph-thrown interception that was returned inside the 10-yard line. The Antelopes lost to Prairie View A&M by a score of 20-7. Pictured below is the coin toss. Howard Hanson (No. 78) is representing the Antelopes while Gov. Frank B. Morrison stands by and observes.

Although the 1963 team members were serious about winning, they still knew how to have a good time. Here some of the guys goof around for the camera. From left to right are Jim Ekerberg, Vaughn Plock, M. C. Crowley, Howard Hansen, and Randy Rasmussen.

Most of coach Allen Zikmund's teams were known for their grinding ground game, but no team was more prolific at running the ball than the 1966 Antelopes. That season, Zikmund's running attack accumulated 3,701 yards to lead the nation in rushing. The offense averaged 370.1 yards per game (still a school record) and set a school record by amassing 599 yards rushing during a 61-6 rout over Chadron. Pictured here is Lannie Shelmadine, who led the team in rushing. Other ball carriers that season included Lee Jacobsen and Rich Osentowski.

Coach Allen Zikmund's Antelopes punished opposing teams with a strong ground attack. Opening holes and blocking for those runners were the men in the trenches, who rarely received recognition in the stats sheets. Ed Kruml (left) was a key player on the offensive line between 1962 and 1965. A four-year letterman at center, Kruml was selected three times to the NCC all-conference team, and in 1965, he was honored as a first-team All-American. Kruml was inducted into the UNK Athletic Hall of Fame in 2003. Pictured below is Gary Welton, a three-year starter at tight end who did much of the blocking for Zikmund's offense. A three-sport letterman in football, basketball, and track, Welton capped his football career with the Carriker Award. Welton was inducted into the UNK Athletic Hall of Fame in 2003.

The most accomplished football player in school history is Randy Rasmussen. As a freshman on the talented 1963 team, Rasmussen was a standout on the defensive line but eventually switched to the offensive side of the ball. Standing 6 feet 1 inch and weighing 270 pounds, Rasmussen opened gaping holes in the opposing line that allowed Kearney's 1966 backfield to lead the nation in rushing. Rasmussen was honored as an All-American, and following his days at Kearney, he went on to have a long career in the NFL, including a Super Bowl title with the New York Jets. Pictured at right is Rasmussen during his college days. Photographed below is Rasmussen as he poses for a photograph at the Blue-Gold scrimmage during his rookie season with the Jets.

In offensive formation, from left to right, is the 1965 offense, players Mike Inselman, Randy Rasmussen, Lonnie Olson, Ed Kruml, Robert Rasmussen, Gary Worrell, and Gary Dubbs. In the backfield are, from left to right, Jerry Stuckert, Lee Jacobsen, quarterback Neil Kaup, and Lannie Shelmadine. In the background one can see the construction of Centennial Towers.

From 1964 to 1965, Neil Kaup quarterbacked the Antelope football team. During the 1965 campaign, he broke the school record for most completions in a season, with 89 passes. Despite this success, the next season Kaup surrendered his starting job to Rich Osentowski. Kaup continued his success on defense, earning first-team all-conference and All-America honors at safety. Pictured here, Kaup is about to spring a long run against Wayne State, while Gary Rasmussen, Randy Rasmussen's older brother, prepares to throw a block.

One of the great multisport athletes in school history, Lee Jacobsen earned four letters each in football, track, and basketball. On the gridiron, Jacobsen played both sides of the ball as a linebacker, fullback, and kicker. He was one of the most prolific scorers in school history. His 266 career points place him second on the all-time scoring list. In 1967, Jacobsen was honored as an All-American linebacker, and in 1968, he was drafted by the New York Jets. He was inducted into the UNK Athletic Hall of Fame in 1987.

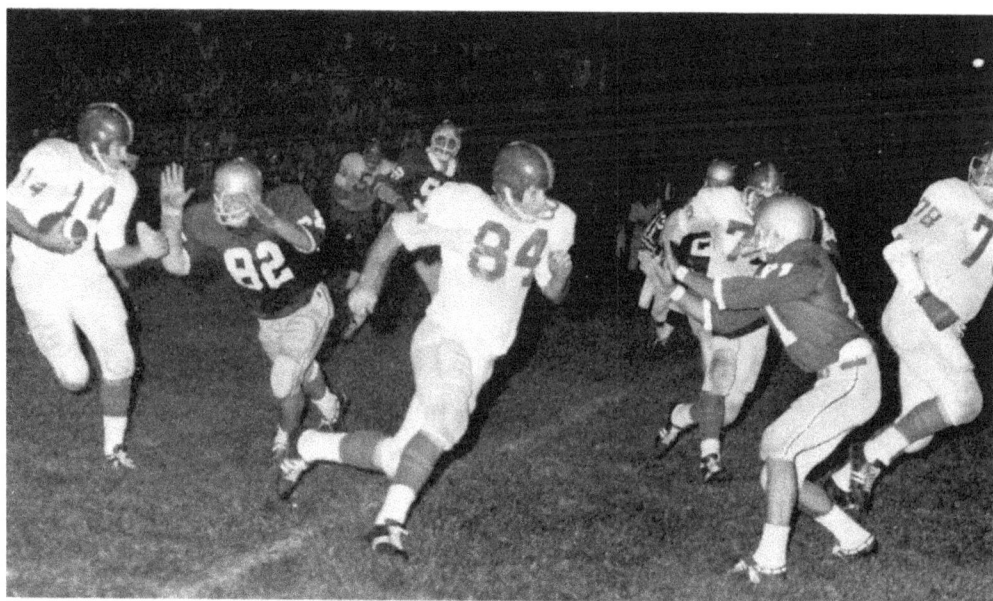

Above, running with the football, is Rich Osentowski. Although he never surpassed his achievements on the baseball diamond, Osentowski served as the signal caller on the 1966 team and was named to the honorable mention All-America list that year. Here, in a 1968 game, Osentowski is trying to turn the corner against the hard-nosed Hastings defense. Worth noting is the fact that he finished the game despite suffering a painful thumb injury, as evidenced in the heavy bandage on his left hand. The 34-20 victory over Hastings was the last time the two schools played.

Greg Cheng (No. 40) kicked two of the longest field goals in Antelope football history. On November 14, 1970, Cheng booted a 51-yard field goal in a 26-14 victory over Northern State. The longest field goal in school history, a 56-yard strike, was kicked by Travis Parker in 1987.

The father of the legendary Husker fullbacks Joel and Jeff Makovicka, John Makovicka was a star runner between 1967 and 1970. During his senior season, Makovicka racked up 19 touchdowns, a single-season record that has yet to be broken as of 2007. He is also number one all-time in career yards per game (148.3). Dr. L. R. Smith, who served as the team physician for nearly 40 years, still believes that Makovicka is the most underrated football player that he had the pleasure of watching. Of Makovicka, Smith said, "He was really a bull." Makovicka was inducted into the UNK Athletic Hall of Fame in 1986.

Jim Zikmund (No. 10), the son of coach Allen Zikmund, was arguably the best pass defender in school history. His 14 interceptions in one season still stand among the best in NAIA history. In 1971, Zikmund was drafted by the Boston Patriots, but an injury prevented him from playing in the professional ranks. Zikmund was named an honorable mention All-American in 1969 and 1970, and he was inducted in the UNK Athletic Hall of Fame in 1998. Jim Jefferies (No. 79) played defensive tackle and was an honorable mention All-American in 1972.

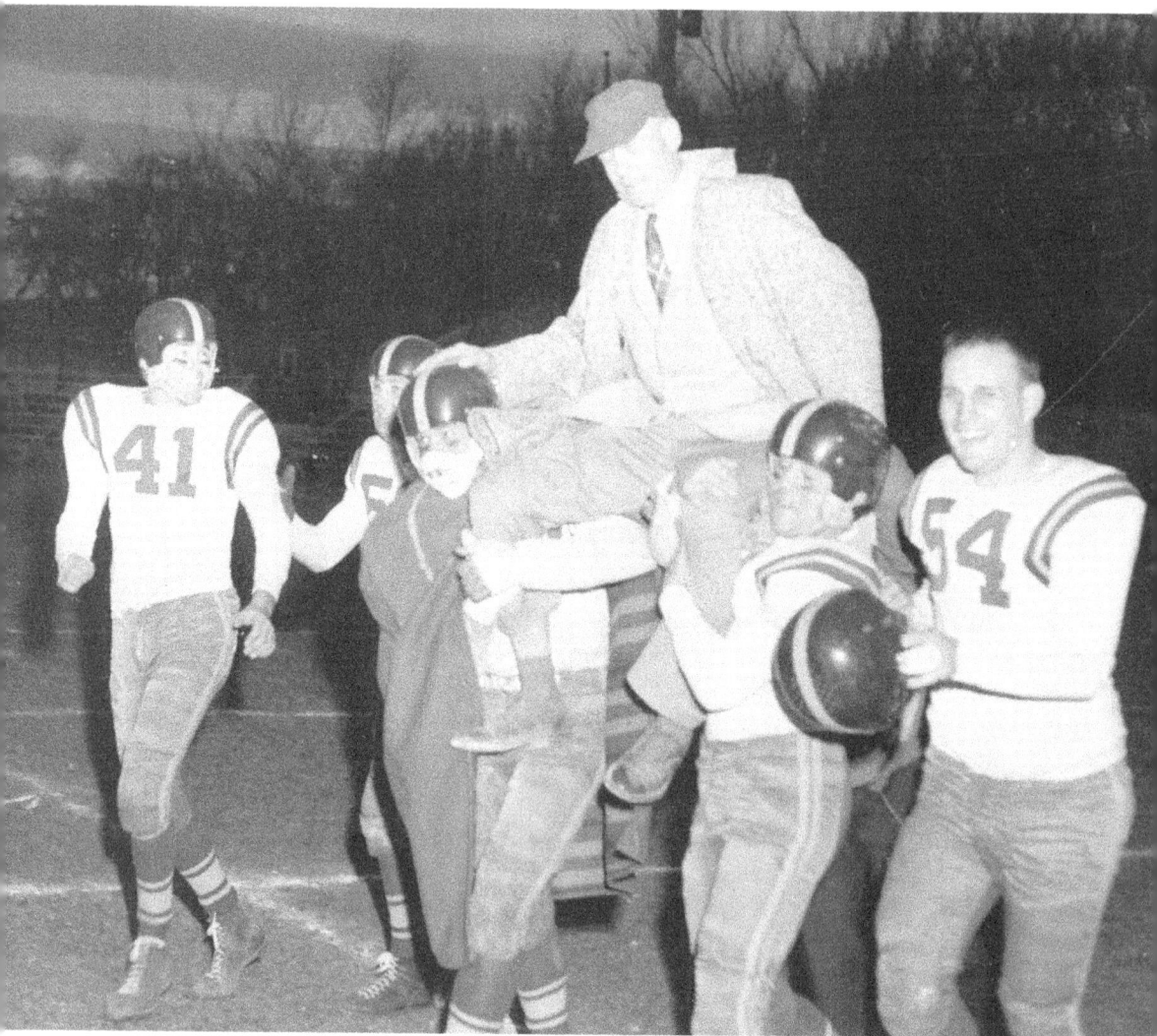

In his 17 years at the helm, coach Allen Zikmund amassed an impressive 121-32-3 record. Zikmund won 78 percent of his games, giving him the highest winning percentage in Kearney football history. Pleasing to the Blue and Gold faithful, under Zikmund's guidance the Antelopes finally managed to gain the upper hand on their archrivals. In his 14 contests against the Hastings Broncos, "Zik" won 12 of 14. After handing coaching duties over to assistant coach Claire Boroff, Zikmund served as athletic director until his retirement in 1987. Zikmund was twice named the State College Coach of the Year, and he has been inducted into the NAIA Hall of Fame, Nebraska Football Hall of Fame, and UNK Athletic Hall of Fame. In this photograph, Zik's players fittingly carry him off the field after a convincing 34-14 victory against Northern State in the Botany Bowl.

5

THE MODERN ERA

1971–2007

A new era, the modern era, began during the 1970s when a slew of coaching changes, the introduction of competitive women's sports, and the eventual move from NAIA to National Collegiate Athletic Association (NCAA) Division II competition forever changed the Antelope athletic program. Charlie Foster's retirement set off a chain reaction that saw Allen Zikmund, Foster's replacement, hand over football coaching duties to former player Claire Boroff. Other coaching changes during the 1970s saw Jerry Hueser take over the basketball team, launching the program into a period of winning that continues today. Guy Murray took over the baseball team in 1972 and over the next 29 seasons amassed 639 wins. Jack Ramey headed the wrestling team throughout the 1970s and 1980s, putting together a program that in the 21st century is one of the best in the nation.

The most visible change, however, was the introduction of competitive women's sports. Although women's athletic teams were organized in the 1960s, it was not until the 1972 passage of Title IX that women had an equal opportunity to compete at the collegiate level. Title IX had an immediate impact. By the 1980s, the women's track, basketball, volleyball, and softball teams were competing at the national level, and in the case of softball, winning national championships. With the move to NCAA Division II, the women's teams have only gotten better. During the first decade of the 21st century, the volleyball team has been consistently ranked in the top 10 in the nation and produces All-Americans on a regular basis, including Erin Gudmundson, the 2004 national player of the year.

Jerry Hueser (pictured at left) took over the basketball program in 1971, and he soon became the most successful basketball coach in school history. During his 26 seasons, he produced a 519-256 record. Included in those years were a number of fantastic teams and memorable seasons. His 1977–1978 team took the NAIA tournament by surprise and upset four top-10 seeds on its way to finishing as the national runner-up. Another of Hueser's outstanding teams was the 1981–1982 squad that lost in the NAIA national semifinal game.

In this photograph, Hueser presents All-American Tom Kropp with an award. Hueser, a UNK Athletic Hall of Fame member, handed coaching duties over to Kropp, his former star player and assistant coach, in 1996. Under Kropp, the basketball program has continued its winning ways. Kropp has taken his teams to the NCAA Division II tournament nine times, including six straight between 2002 and 2007.

The 1974–1975 team was led by Tom Kropp and Loren Killion, who helped guide the team to a 21-7 record. The team reached the NAIA playoffs but lost in the first round 94-86 to Fairmont State. As a super sophomore, Loren Killion (No. 41) was one of the standouts that year. During his career, Killion amassed a total of 2,100 points, an amount that, as of 2007, placed him third all-time. In 1977, Killion was named an All-American, and in 1989, he was inducted into the athletic hall of fame.

The most polished basketball player in school history, Tom Kropp (No. 50) was named a first-team All-American in 1975. Kropp owns the school record for points in a game, which he set against Central Missouri State in 1974 when he poured in 51 points. He is also second in rebounds and fifth in career points. Kropp was drafted by the NBA's Washington Bullets in 1975. After several seasons in the NBA, Kropp spent the rest of his career playing in Belgium. Among many other honors, Kropp is a member of the UNK, Nebraska Football, NAIA, and Nebraska High School Halls of Fame.

Above are the members of the 1977–1978 "Cinderella" basketball team. From left to right are (first row) Tom Ritzdorf, Rick Hook, Dave Hahn, and Tim Mohanna; (second row) Randy Cipriano, Gregg Grubaugh, Tim Higgins, Bruce Hird, Ken Adkisson, Pat Lynch, and Mark Etzelmiller. Finishing as the national runner-up, the team made a magical run through the NAIA postseason tournament by defeating top-ranked teams like Mercyhurst College, the University of Wisconsin–Parkside, Winston-Salem State, and Quincy College. Coming up just short of a national championship, the team's four-point loss to Grand Canyon College was described by observers as the most memorable game in the tournament's history. Pictured below are key players with the runner-up trophy. From left to right are Tom Ritzdorf (tournament MVP), Dave Hahn, and coach Jerry Hueser.

Bart Kofoed, a transfer from Hastings College, was probably the most talented offensive basketball player in school history. During his senior season, he set a number of records that have yet to be broken. Among others, he owns the records in points per game in a season (26.5), points in a season (902), assists in a season (198), and field goals made in a season (358). Kofoed was drafted in the fifth round by the Utah Jazz, for whom he played parts of two seasons. Kofoed also played for the Golden State Warriors, Seattle Supersonics, and Boston Celtics. In 2000, Kofoed was inducted into the UNK Athletic Hall of Fame.

In 1999, Eric Strand surpassed 1970s scoring ace Loren Killion to become the all-time leading Loper scorer. Between 1995 and 1999, Strand scored 2,173 total points. Since his graduation, Strand has been playing professionally in numerous locations around the world. Honored as an All-American in 1998 and 1999, Strand was the first Loper cager to earn that honor twice. Other All-Americans during the modern era include Bart Kofoed, Jon Bergmeier, Doug Holtmeier, Tim Higgins, Loren Killion, Tom Kropp, Nick Svehla, Nick Branting, and Dusty Jura.

Coach Tom Kropp's most successful team was the talent-laden 2002–2003 squad. That team made the school's first-ever appearance in the NCAA Division II Elite Eight. Pictured above is an emotional Nick Svehla with coach Kevin Lofton. Just moments prior to this photograph, Svehla, a two-time All-American, hit one of the most memorable shots in school history to beat Metro State in double overtime to advance to the Elite Eight. At left is All-American teammate Nick Branting, who during his senior season was named the Division II Player of the Year.

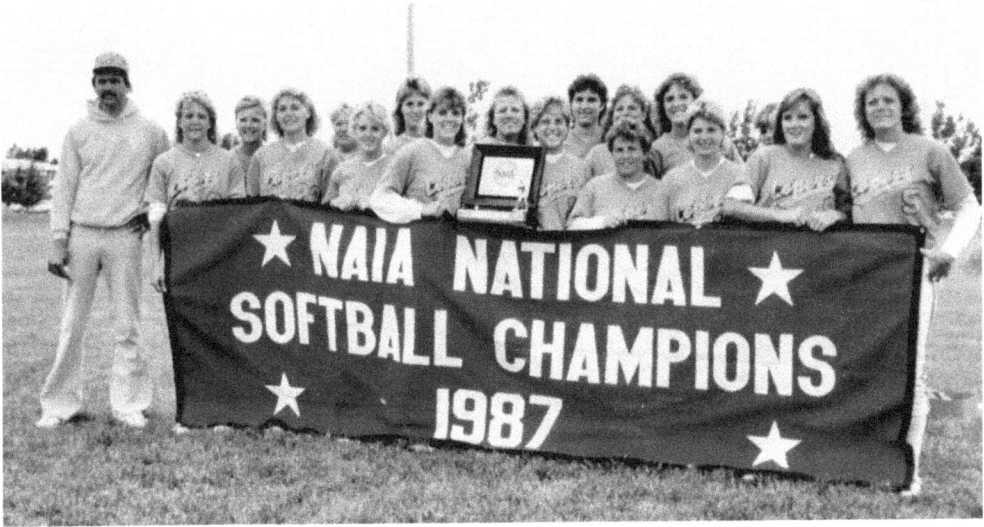

During the modern era, softball became one of the most successful Loper sports programs. Between 1981 and 1990, the Lady Lopers played in nine NAIA national tournaments and captured national championships in 1987 and 1990. Pictured here is the 1987 national championship team that ran roughshod over the competition at the national tournament held in Kearney. Since moving to Division II in 1991, the Loper softball team has regularly appeared in postseason play, finishing as high as second in 1999.

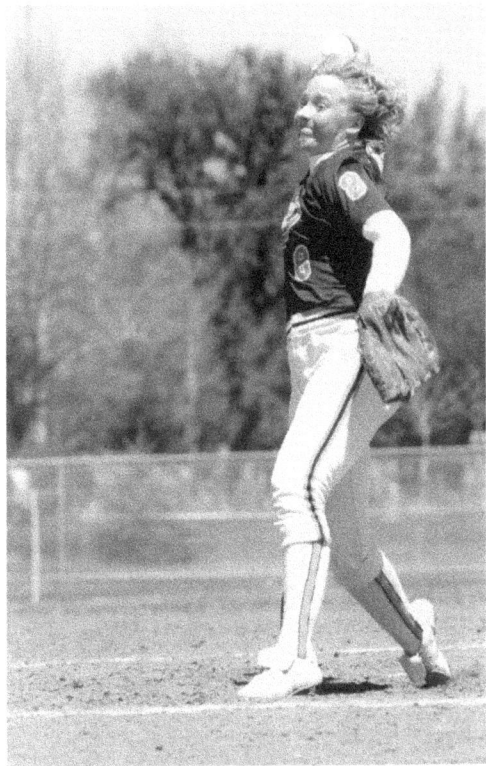

Susan Johnson was one of the most decorated softball players in school history. A two-time All-American, Johnson was named the NCAA Woman of the Year in 1992. In her career, she struck out more than 920 batters, still good enough, as of 2000, to rank her fourth all-time in NCAA Division II history. Johnson also owns the school record for career wins, with 85, and career ERA, a stingy 0.62.

Pictured here is two-time All-American Amanda Kelly. A dominant pitcher between 1997 and 2000, Kelly holds numerous records, including the all-time highest winning percentage (61 wins and 9 losses), and is third in strikeouts (631) and ERA (1.14). Other talented players were Holly Waller (Carnes), who has coached the Lady Lopers since 2001, Phyllis DeBuhr, a three-time All-American and star pitcher of the 1987 champion team, All-Americans Brenda Gonnerman, Michelle Cudderford, Kathy Nelson, Nancy Loescher, Kris McMullen, Kelly Moats, Darcie Berry, and standouts LaNell Cox, Jill McCaslin, and Becky Sintek.

Basketball coach Joe Sanchez led the Lady Lopers to a 19-9 record and a berth in the 1994 NCAA tournament, the first such appearance in school history. That squad was led by Ginger Keller (left), arguably the best female basketball player in school history. Keller, a 2006 inductee to the UNK Athletic Hall of Fame, still holds the school record in career points, rebounds per game, and free throws made. Other notable players during the modern era were honorable mention All-Americans LaNell Cox, who was also a standout on the softball team, first-team All-American Darcy Stracke, Jessica Kedrowski, Cathy Wier, All-American Beth Swift, Allison Kruger, and Kalee Modlin.

THE MODERN ERA

In eight seasons, Amy Stephens complied an 83.7 percent winning percentage. The best team during that stretch was the 1996–1997 squad, which finished a school best 28-3. The team lost in the second round of the NCAA Division II tournament to North Dakota State. Also impressive is the NCAA Division II record 87-game home win streak that was intact between 1995 and 2001. In 2007, the program is under the leadership of coach Carol Russell. Pictured above is the 1986–1987 team, the first team to play in a postseason tournament. One of the standouts on that team was LaNell Cox (No. 30). Below is coach Amy Stephens, as she cuts down the net.

For 24 years, Rosella Meier (top row, far right) coached the Antelope volleyball teams. Winning 73 percent of her matches, Meier had a number of outstanding teams, including the 1980–1982 era, when her teams finished third, seventh, and fourth at the NAIA national championships. Playing as an independent in 1990, her team went 40-1. In 1993, Patty Sitorius took over, and she did her best to replace Meier, a legend, by guiding the program to two NCAA Elite Eight appearances in 1995 and 1996.

Since 1999, Rick Squiers has guided the Loper volleyball team to the NCAA tournament every year. In 2004, the volleyball team finished the season with a record of 40-1, with the one loss coming in the national semifinal game of the NCAA tournament. In 2005, the team continued its exceptional ways by going 38-2 and finishing as the national runner-up. Pictured here, Erin Gudmundson (No. 11) and teammates celebrate a point during the 2005 national championship game held in Kearney.

Ten volleyball players have earned All-America honors. Amy Anderson (pictured above), who played for Meier during the late 1980s, was an All-American in 1988. Pictured below from left to right are Erin Gudmundson, Erin Arnold, and Erin Brosz, who played together between 2002 and 2004. Sometimes called the "Three Erins," their names dominate the UNK volleyball record books. Erin Brosz, who appears on the all-time list in kills and owns the school record in career hitting percentage, was an All-American in 2004 and 2005. Erin Arnold, an All-American in 2003 and 2004, is number two in career kills, attack attempts, and service aces. Erin Gudmundson is arguably the finest volleyball player in school history. She finished her career as a three-time All-American and the 2005 American Volleyball Coaches Association (AVCA) Division II National Player of the Year. Rounding out the list of All-Americans are Danielle Shum, Bethany Spilde, Diane Davidson, Samantha Harvey, Kelli Brummer, and Angie Janicek Reed.

Jack Ramey headed the wrestling team through most of the 1970s and 1980s. Under his guidance, 16 Lopers earned All-America honors, including three-time All-American Dean Reicks. In 1987, Ed Scantling took over coaching duties and lifted the program to new heights. In 1990, he coached two Lopers to national championships: Brian Hagan won at 118 pounds, and Ali Amiri-Eliasi (now known as Ali Elias) took home the gold in the 150-pound weight class. Amiri-Eliasi (pictured here), a native of Iran, captured another championship in 1991 and went on to finish his career as Kearney's first four-time All-American wrestler. He was inducted into the UNK Athletic Hall of Fame in 2004.

In very recent years, Kearney has become a wrestling powerhouse of sorts. Coached by Marc Bauer, the UNK wrestling program regularly produces All-Americans. One of the many outstanding wrestlers was Jeff Sylvester, a four-time All-American and national champion at 197 pounds in 2004.

THE MODERN ERA

Tervel Dlagnev won the 2007 heavyweight national title. Dlagnev, along with his national champion teammate Trevor Charbonneau (125 pounds), led the way in capturing the national runner-up team title at the 2007 national championship that was held at UNK. Other national champions in school history are Brian Hagan (118 pounds), Ali Amiri-Eliasi (150 pounds), who in 2007 was inducted into the NCAA Hall of Fame, Frank Kuchera (174 pounds), Brett Allgood (133 pounds), and Tanner Linsacum (184 pounds).

Bryce Abbey is one of three Loper grapplers to earn All-America honors four times (Ali Amiri-Eliasi and Jeff Sylvester are the other two). Wrestling at 125 pounds, Abbey placed fourth, third, third, and fifth at the national meet. Other noteworthy grapplers were Martin Segovia, a three-time All-American who twice finished in second place, and three-time All American Brandon Pfizenmaier, who was the national runner-up in 2003.

With the passage of Title IX in 1972, collegiate athletics for women became more common. Although forced into retirement, coach Charlie Foster organized a women's track team during the early 1970s. By the late 1970s, coach Mary Iten joined the coaching staff and "Charlie's Angels," as the women's track team was known, dominated collegiate competition at the conference and regional level and routinely sent competitors to the national meet. Marilyn Dubbs (pictured here with Foster) was the first Nebraska female to clear six feet in the high jump. She twice took first place at the prestigious Drake Relays and she was named an Association for Intercollegiate Athletics for Women (AIAW) All-American after finishing fourth and third at the national meet in 1975 and 1976. Dubbs was inducted into the UNK Athletic Hall of Fame in 1988.

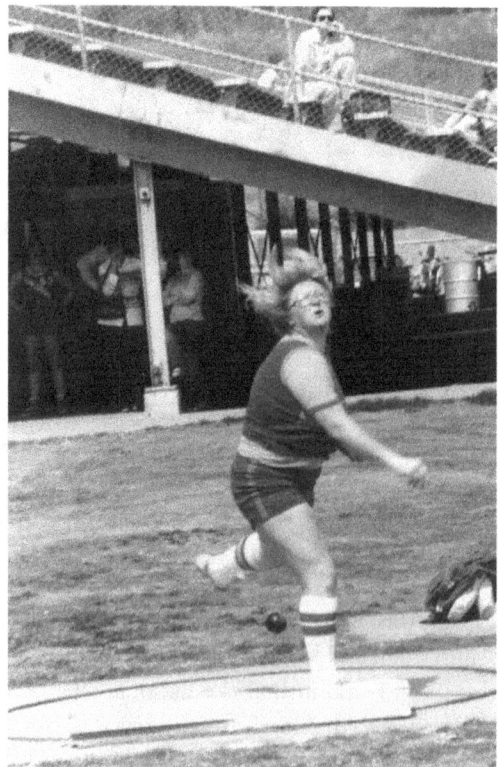

Jill Stenwall was the first of "Charlie's Angels" to win a national championship. In 1980, she captured the AIAW indoor shot put championship. Not only was she a national champion, but in 1980, she was ranked sixth in the entire nation. Although Stenwall qualified for the 1980 Olympic trials, injury prevented her from competing. Her best put of 51 feet and 5.25 inches is still the school record as of 2007. Stenwall was inducted into the athletic hall of fame in 1996.

THE MODERN ERA

Donna Spickelmier was the most dominating female distance runner in school history. Running track and cross-country between 1986 and 1990, Spickelmier won five national championships and earned eight All-America honors in track. In 1987, she captured the indoor mile, setting a national record with a time of 4:57.78. Spickelmier's best year was 1989 when she won outdoor titles in the 1,500 and 3,000 meters. In cross-country, Spickelmier earned three All-America honors and finished third in the nation as a senior. As of 2007, Spickelmier still holds six school records. Spickelmier was inducted into the UNK Athletic Hall of Fame in 2001. Pictured with Spickelmier is coach Mary Iten.

Beth Stuart is the most decorated athlete in school history. She dominated the shot put and discus during the mid-1980s, earning 12 All-America honors and seven national titles. During her senior year in 1987, Stuart was the indoor national champion in the shot and the outdoor champion in both discus and shot. Stuart capped her career by being named the 1987 Nebraska College Athlete of the Year. She was inducted into the UNK Athletic Hall of Fame in 1998. Stuart is pictured here on the podium with one of her seven national championship awards.

The tradition of great Kearney pole-vaulters continued during the modern era. Pictured above is Mike Ford with his parents, Bill and Martha Ford. Ford, who just missed taking home a Division II national title in 2005, owns both the indoor and outdoor school pole vault records. His best vault was 17 feet and 2.75 inches. Ford and his parents invented the Swing-Up Invert Machine, a device that is used to help vaulters perfect their technique. After volunteering for a number of years, Bill and Martha Ford are now the official pole vault coaches at UNK.

One of the most talented father-son tandems in school history is Ron and John Laux. Ron, who was a star jumper and football player for Kearney in the late 1960s, is a member of the UNK Athletic Hall of Fame. His son John, it has been said, is a chip off the old block. After breaking the 50-foot barrier for the first time in school history, John went on to break every triple jump record at UNK. In 2003, he had the best jump of his career when he went 50 feet and 5 inches.

THE MODERN ERA

Lance Pfeiffer continued the tradition of great Loper shot putters by capturing two national titles. In 2006, he won the outdoor crown, while in 2007, he was the indoor champion. He owns the school record of 61 feet 2.75 inches. Pfeiffer is one of only three Loper men to win two national titles in track (Clayton Scott and Jim Sobieszczyk are the others).

Shane Fruit, pictured here, returned the Loper harriers to the days of glory when, in 1980, he earned All-America honors. Thereafter, other Loper harriers began making an impact. Dan Pavlik (1983), Mike Hamm (1984), and Dale Mackel (1984) earned All-America status. In 1991, the Lopers finished second in the nation, while in 1992 and 1993, they finished third and fourth, respectively. Standout runners during this period included Bobby Brindamour, Tom Magnusson, and Joe Schumm, each earning All-America honors at the national meet. Bulgarian-born Ivan Ivanov, who placed sixth in the nation in 1994 and fourth in 1995, was perhaps the best runner to compete for the Lopers since the days of Larry Snell, Tuck Mason, and Gary Shubert.

Stability was brought to the baseball program in 1972 when Guy Murray took over the program. Murray coached the baseball team for a record 29 seasons, compiling 639 wins. To prepare his team for conference play, every spring Murray took his teams into Texas and Oklahoma, where the Lopers faced Division I teams. In 1999, Murray was inducted into the American Baseball Coaches Hall of Fame, and in 2007, he was inducted into the UNK Athletic Hall of Fame. Notable players during the Murray era include Ken Vergith, Mitch Johnson, and Chuck Schnoor.

Ken Vergith (far left) was one of the most dominating pitchers during the Murray era. Armed with a nearly unhittable slider, Vergith, who pitched between 1973 and 1976, still decorates the baseball record books. He is the career leader in wins, with 22, and, as of 2007, is still ranked second in strikeouts with 242. Vergith's impressive 2.56 career ERA places him third on the career best list. In 1976, he threw eight complete games (tied for first on the all-time list). Vergith tossed three no-hitters during his career, and in 1975, he earned All-America honors. Vergith was inducted into the UNK Athletic Hall of Fame in 1998.

Between 1977 and 1988, Murray took four of his teams to Hawaii. The Loper baseball squad faced top-rated teams such as the University of Southern California, Florida State, the University of Hawaii, and the University of Nevada, Las Vegas. Such competition helped prepare the Loper baseball squad for its conference schedule. Playing such stiff spring competition, Murray's baseball squads won 10 of 16 NAIA district championships. Standing in Rainbow Stadium are the senior members of the 1980 team. From left to right are Chuck Schnoor, Dennis Lewis, Craig "Doc" Fundum, Rob Mohon, Todd Higgans, and Bill Becker.

Above is star Loper slugger Bronson Bosshammer. Between 1996 and 1999, Bosshammer "hammered" his way into the school record books. In 1998, he finished the season with a .465 batting average, an average that still stands as the second best in school history. All-time, he is third in career hits, first in doubles, first in total extra-base hits, second in total bases, third in RBIs, and fifth in home runs.

Pictured here is coach Claire Boroff with Scott Maline, quarterback for the 1973 Lopers and an honorable mention All-American. Boroff, who replaced coach Allen Zikmund in 1972, continued Kearney's winning tradition. His Loper teams won conference championships (or were cochampions) every year between 1972 and 1980. During 28 seasons at the helm, Boroff amassed an impressive 169-105-5 record, placing him at the top of the all-time win list. Since 2000, Darrell Morris has headed the Loper football program.

Tom Kropp is arguably the most talented athlete to come out of Kearney. A multisport star, Kropp earned All-America status in both football and basketball. In football, he began his career on offense, but after recovering from an injury, he switched to linebacker during his senior year. In 1974, Kropp earned All-America honors and was drafted by the NFL's Pittsburgh Steelers in the eighth round.

Pictured here are Phil Gustafson (standing) and Kirk Heyer. Gustafson, from Galesburg, Illinois, transferred from Notre Dame and in 1973 earned first-team All-America status as a defensive lineman. Heyer earned honorable mention All-America status in 1974 for his defensive play. Other All-Americans from the 1970s include Randy Nelson, Tom Kropp, Mitch Johnson, Bill Windhorst, Doug Petersen, Tom Virgil, and Mike McGlade.

Boroff had many fine teams, but the 1980 team was his only team to advance past the first round of the NAIA playoffs. Ending the regular season with an 8-1-1 record and a conference championship, the Lopers earned a spot in the NAIA playoffs. The first round saw the squad travel to North Carolina, where it earned a hard-fought 9-6 overtime victory against Mars Hill College. The Lopers stumbled in the second round, though, losing 14-0 against a tough Northeastern State University team. Pictured here from left to right are team leaders Jay Bergmeier, Dan Boomhower, Dean Carstens, Mark Lundeen, and Steve Dunn.

Between 1972 and 1987, 49 Lopers were selected to NAIA All-America lists. Two Lopers, Scott Schug (kicker) and Roger Wachholtz (defensive line) earned two selections. As the above photograph suggests, Roger Wachholtz, a four-year letterman between 1974 and 1977, was a fierce defensive player. Wachholtz earned All-America honors in 1976 (second team) and 1977 (first team). Scot Schug was a three-year letterman between 1980 and 1982 and earned All-America first-team honors in 1981 and 1982. Schug led the nation in punting in 1981 with a 44.8-yard average. During the first round of the 1980 NAIA playoffs against Mars Hill, Schug's leg kept the Lopers in the game by pinning the Lions deep in their own territory. Schug was inducted into the athletic hall of fame in 2001.

Coach Claire Boroff continued to produce All-Americans in the 1980s. Jeff Norblade earned All-America honors in 1987 as a defensive back. During his senior season, Norblade nabbed seven interceptions, returning three for touchdowns. One of those interceptions he ran back 78 yards for a touchdown, setting a school record. Norblade was inducted into the athletic hall of fame in 2002. Other All-Americans during the 1980s include Jeff Stenslokken, Jerry Scott, Burt Muehling, Jon Gustafson, and Troy Stonacek.

Justin Coleman, who was the runner-up for the Harlon Hill Trophy (given to the Division II national player of the year) in 2000, finished his career as Kearney's most outstanding passing quarterback. With 11,213 career passing yards, Coleman has 5,200 more yards than Pat Korth, who is second all time. Coleman's 99 career touchdown passes are also more than twice that of any other Loper in school history. His highest one-game total was against Wayne State in 1999, when he threw for 483 yards and six touchdowns. As a barometer of his success, Coleman finished his career with more collegiate passing yards than Peyton Manning or Doug Flutie.

A CENTURY OF SPORTS

Pictured is running back Mike Miller. Miller, who played for the Lopers from 2001 to 2004, is the school's all-time rushing leader. He concluded his career with 4,818 yards. In 2002, he was named an All-American and Rocky Mountain Athletic Conference (RMAC) Offensive Player of the Year. He also has the most rushing touchdowns in school history, with 34 feathers in his cap.

Pictured above is Richie Ross, as he hauls in yet another pass. Ross, who played for UNK from 2002 to 2005, is the best receiver in school history. He finished his career with a school record 279 receptions and 4,882 yards receiving. With 50 touchdowns, Ross also owns the most touchdowns in school history. Following his Antelope playing days, in 2006 Ross played in a number of preseason games for the NFL's Houston Texans. He then finished the season with the Tennessee Titans.

THE MODERN ERA

As UNK moves on from its centennial anniversary, the sports programs in recent years have reached an unforeseen level of success and recognition. Besides winning the Wells Fargo Cup—the trophy (right) given to the all-sports champion of the RMAC conference—for an unprecedented 11 years straight, UNK's Health and Sports Center has also been home to a number of NCAA championships. For instance, in the last half decade UNK has hosted the men's basketball regional, the women's volleyball and basketball national championships, and the wrestling championship. In recent years, UNK has had the largest average attendance among all Division II teams in volleyball and men's basketball. It has also frequently been in the top 10 in women's basketball. In the photograph below is another packed house.

Visit us at
arcadiapublishing.com

www.ingramcontent.com/pod-product-compliance
Lightning Source LLC
Chambersburg PA
CBHW080608110426
42813CB00006B/1444